The
SURVIVOR

24 Spine-Chilling Adventures on the Edge of Death

John Goddard

Health Communications, Inc.
Deerfield Beach, Florida

www.hci-online.com

Library of Congress Cataloging-in-Publication Data

Goddard, John
The survivor : 24 spine-chilling adventures on the edge of death /
 John Goddard.
    p.   cm.
  ISBN 1-55874-695-1 (tradepaper)
   1. Goddard, John—Journeys. 2. Adventure and adventurers—
United States—Biography. 3. Risk-taking (Psychology) I. Title.

CT99712.G63 A3 2001
904—dc21

              2001024099

Publisher: Health Communications, Inc.
         3201 S.W. 15th Street
         Deerfield Beach, FL 33442-8190

Cover design by Larissa Hise Henoch
Inside book design by Lawna Patterson Oldfield
Cover artwork appeared in the October 1983 issue of Reader's Digest.

This book is dedicated to my wife, Carol, whose wise counsel, infinite patience and steadfast encouragement have contributed so greatly to the writing of this book, and to our wonderful children, Lisa, Jonelle, Jeffery, Stewart, Julie and Tera, for their enthusiastic support.

EDITOR'S NOTE

This book was written entirely by the author, who endeavored to describe each event in a straightforward style without exaggeration or embellishment. It is a compilation of twenty-four of the most life-threatening of his adventures.

CONTENTS

ACKNOWLEDGMENTS

I am deeply grateful to our children, for their sustaining love and encouragement throughout the writing of the book, and to my wife, Carol, for her vital contribution as an insightful sounding board; she was able to unlock details of the "close calls" that have enhanced each story from my storehouse of memories.

I give special thanks to a number of friends whose unfailing support and beneficial suggestions contributed to the completion of the book, especially my lifelong friends, Ardean and Elna Watts of Salt Lake City, Utah, and Colin and Kathy Sandell of Cedarburg, Wisconsin. Also important were Maria Dales, tireless animal advocate and lover and protector of all living creatures large and small, and David Alexander, gifted writer who authored the definitive biography of the originator of *Star Trek*, Gene Roddenberry.

My heartfelt appreciation to Mark Victor Hansen, co-creator of the bestselling *Chicken Soup for the Soul* series, for his invaluable advice and the empowering inspiration provided by him. He is a man I'm proud to regard as a close friend and the most dynamic motivator I know.

My gratitude also for the endeavors of the talented staff at Health Communications, particularly the generosity of president Peter Vegso; the editorial guidance of Christine Belleris and Allison Janse; the creativity of Larissa Hise Henoch and her associates in the art department; as well as the enthusiasm of the sales and publicity staff.

My thanks to Dawn Aberg and Katie Siegal for efficiently transcribing the chapters into professional form and for being undaunted and uncomplaining, even though having to frequently decipher my last-minute, handwritten additions to the narratives.

PREFACE

From early childhood I had always dreamed of becoming an explorer. According to my parents, Jack and Lettie Goddard, I first expressed this desire when one of my mother's five brothers, Cecil Sorenson, asked me what I wanted to be when I grew up. Without hesitation I answered, "Explorer!" I was five years old at the time. Somehow I had acquired the impression that an explorer was someone who lived in the jungle with natives and lots of wild animals, and I couldn't imagine anything better than that! Unlike other little boys, most of whom changed their minds about what they want to be several times as they grew older, I never wavered from this ambition.

Though I was an only child and therefore could have led a sheltered life with overly protective parents, I was blessed with an enlightened mother and father who recognized early on that they had a son who was unconventional in many ways. Instead of squelching my innate love of nature and wildlife and my desire to become an explorer, they bought me a little pith helmet and canteen and took me on frequent camping trips to the wilderness areas of California and Utah.

I was never happier than when taking long hikes through a forest or along the banks of lakes and streams, quietly observing the birds and animals there. I particularly enjoyed summertime, when school was out. Then I could escape the suffocating urban life in the city of Los Angeles and work on my Uncle Royal's big cattle and sheep ranch in Idaho. Each summer, from the age of ten until I joined the air force at eighteen, I lived the rugged but rewarding life of a ranch hand.

Uncle Royal's ranch was a wildlife paradise, consisting of more than six thousand uninhabited acres of the most varied terrain in Idaho. The Snake River flowed through the eastern section of his spread, with abundant beaver, muskrats and waterfowl, and even a colony of elegant white ibis along the banks.

To the north was a semidesert, with the flora and fauna characteristic of this type of region. The rest of the land consisted of broad plains, unexplored woods and lush fields of alfalfa. Nor far from the ranch house were two ancient volcanic cones, where I found well-preserved Indian petroglyphs and beautifully chiseled obsidian arrowheads.

On weekdays I worked from dawn to dusk, along with my older cousin Hugh and the other ranch hands—milking cows, rounding up stray cattle, building and mending fences, raking and stacking the fragrant alfalfa, digging irrigation canals and a dozen other chores, such as feeding the four big sheepdogs and weeding my Aunt Ruth's capacious vegetable garden.

Uncle Royal gave the impression of a gruff and somewhat irascible overseer. But as we worked together with the livestock and in the fields, I discovered that he had a gentle side and a surprisingly deep concern for birds and animals that matched my own. He was one of the dominant influences of my boyhood, and I admired him greatly.

The weekends were largely mine to enjoy on my own. I usually took off for day-long rambles on foot or riding on "Major," the splendid Morgan horse my uncle had given me. I loved exploring all areas of the vast ranch, encountering wildlife everywhere I traveled, from weasels, badgers and porcupines to deer and coyotes. There was also an abundance of birds, including golden eagles, grouse, pheasant, chukar partridge, Canadian geese and various waterfowl.

In addition to working on Uncle Royal's ranch, I worked for two weeks each summer on the southern Idaho wheat farm of two other uncles, Cecil and Pierre. Here, I enjoyed two of the proudest moments of my boyhood when, at the age of ten, my Uncle Pierre taught me how to drive a tractor and then, the following summer, Uncle Cecil instructed me on driving the farm truck.

I still recall my anxiety when my uncles gave me chores

that seemed beyond my years and abilities. In spite of that, I was eager to prove that even a "city kid" could be really useful to them.

By following their instructions and those of the ranch hands, I gradually was able to handle each work assignment they gave me. Though the endless manual labor, at both the ranch and the dry farm, was hot and exhausting, I was always sorry to come to the end of summer. But I returned home each time physically stronger, with increased self-confidence and a greater sense of independence. From the beginning, the arduous work and being entrusted with important responsibilities despite my youth helped me develop a deep-seated sense of discipline, perseverance and the satisfaction that comes in doing a job to the best of one's ability—qualities that were invaluable throughout my life, particularly in carrying out the number-one goal of my life: exploring the world's longest river, the 4,220-mile Nile (see chapter 10).

When I was in the fifth grade, I began a lifelong love of reading. Each Monday after school, I would check out three or four books from our library, read them by the end of the week and then be ready for more.

Several subjects interested me, but particularly world geography and the unusual places and people an explorer might want to visit.

As I grew older and expanded my reading, I repeatedly came upon references to the Nile as the most important river on Earth, the one that has, for the past six thousand years, had the greatest influence on the development of civilization—agriculture, writing, law, the arts, architecture, even astronomy and religion.

By the time I reached the age of fifteen, I had become firmly convinced that exploring the Nile was the most exciting and deeply challenging project I could choose in my career as an explorer.

One rainy afternoon I sat down at my kitchen table and wrote three words at the top of a yellow pad, "My Life List." Under that heading I wrote down 127 goals. Since then I have completed 111 of those goals and expanded the list to more than 500. My goals included climbing the world's major mountains, exploring vast waterways, running a mile in five minutes, reading the complete works of Shakespeare and graduating from the University of Southern California.

Explore:
✓ 1. Nile River
✓ 2. Amazon River
✓ 3. Congo River
✓ 4. Colorado River
   5. Yangtze River, China
   6. Niger River
   7. Orinoco River, Venezuela
✓ 8. Rio Coco, Nicaragua
✓ 9. The Congo
✓ 10. New Guinea
✓ 11. Brazil
✓ 12. Borneo
✓ 13. The Sudan (I was nearly buried alive in a sandstorm.)

Study Tribal Cultures In:
✓ 14. Australia
✓ 15. Kenya
✓ 16. The Philippines
✓ 17. Tanganyika (now Tanzania)
✓ 18. Ethiopia
✓ 19. Nigeria
✓ 20. Alaska

Climb:
   21. Mount Everest
   22. Mount Aconcagua, Argentina
   23. Mount McKinley
✓ 24. Mount Huascaran, Peru

Climb (cont'd):

✓ 25. Mount Kilimanjaro (twice)
✓ 26. Mount Ararat, Turkey
✓ 27. Mount Kenya
   28. Mount Cook, New Zealand
✓ 29. Mount Popocatepetl, Mexico
✓ 30. The Matterhorn
✓ 31. Mount Rainier
✓ 32. Mount Fuji
✓ 33. Mount Vesuvius
✓ 34. Mount Bromo, Java
✓ 35. Grand Tetons
✓ 36. Mount Baldy, California

✓ 37. Carry out careers in medicine and exploration (studied pre-med and treated simple illnesses among villagers)
   38. Visit every country in the world (visited 122 countries already!)
✓ 39. Study Navaho and Hopi cultures
✓ 40. Learn to fly a plane (have flown 40 different aircraft)
✓ 41. Ride horse in Rose Parade

Photograph:

✓ 42. Iguacu Falls, on Brazil-Argentine border
✓ 43. Victoria Falls, Zimbabwe
✓ 44. Sutherland Falls, New Zealand
✓ 45. Yosemite Falls
✓ 46. Niagara Falls
✓ 47. Retrace travels of Marco Polo and Alexander the Great

Explore Underwater:

✓ 48. Coral reefs of Florida
✓ 49. Great Barrier Reef, Australia (photographed a 300-pound clam)
✓ 50. Red Sea
✓ 51. Fiji Islands
✓ 52. The Bahamas
✓ 53. Explore Okefenokee Swamp and the Everglades

Visit:

   54. North and South Poles
✓ 55. Great Wall of China

✓ 56. Panama and Suez Canals
✓ 57. Easter Island
✓ 58. The Galapagos Islands
✓ 59. Vatican City (saw the pope)
✓ 60. The Taj Mahal
✓ 61. The Eiffel Tower
✓ 62. The Blue Grotto (Isle of Capri, Italy)
✓ 63. The Tower of London
✓ 64. The Leaning Tower of Pisa
✓ 65. The Sacred Well of Chichen-Itza, Mexico
✓ 66. Climb Ayers Rock in Australia
   67. Follow River Jordan from Sea of Galilee to Dead Sea

Swim In:
✓ 68. Lake Victoria
✓ 69. Lake Superior
✓ 70. Lake Tanganyika
✓ 71. Lake Titicaca, Peru
✓ 72. Lake Nicaragua

Accomplish:
✓ 73. Become an Eagle Scout
✓ 74. Dive in a submarine
✓ 75. Land on and take off from an aircraft carrier (8 days aboard the *Independence*)
✓ 76. Fly in a blimp, hot air balloon and glider
✓ 77. Ride an elephant, camel, ostrich and bronco
✓ 78. Skin dive to 40 feet and hold breath two and a half minutes underwater ·
✓ 79. Catch a ten-pound lobster and a ten-inch abalone
✓ 80. Play flute and violin
✓ 81. Type 50 words a minute
✓ 82. Make a parachute jump (have made 17 jumps)
✓ 83. Learn water and snow skiing
✓ 84. Go on a church mission
   85. Follow the John Muir Trail
✓ 86. Study native medicines and bring back useful ones
✓ 87. Bag camera trophies of elephant, lion, rhino, cheetah, cape buffalo and whale

Accomplish (cont'd):

✓ 88. Learn to fence

✓ 89. Learn jujitsu

✓ 90. Teach a college course

✓ 91. Watch a cremation ceremony in Bali

✓ 92. Explore depths of the sea

93. Appear in a Tarzan movie. (I now consider this an irrelevant boyhood dream.)

94. Own a horse, chimpanzee, cheetah, ocelot and coyote (yet to own a chimp or cheetah)

95. Become a ham radio operator

✓ 96. Build own telescope

✓ 97. Write a book on the Nile expedition

✓ 98. Publish an article in *National Geographic* magazine

✓ 99. High jump five feet

✓ 100. Broad jump 15 feet

✓ 101. Run a mile in five minutes

✓ 102. Weigh 175 pounds stripped (still do)

✓ 103. Perform 200 sit-ups and 20 pull-ups

✓ 104. Learn French, Spanish and Arabic

105. Study dragon lizards on Komodo Island (boat broke down within 20 miles of island)

✓ 106. Visit birthplace of Grandfather Sorenson in Denmark

✓ 107. Visit birthplace of Grandfather Goddard in England

✓ 108. Ship aboard a freighter as a seaman

109. Read the entire *Encyclopedia Britannica* (have read extensive parts in each of the 24 volumes)

✓ 110. Read the Bible from cover to cover

✓ 111. Read the works of Shakespeare, Plato, Aristotle, Dickens, Thoreau, Poe, Rousseau, Bacon, Hemingway, Twain, Burroughs, Conrad, Talmage, Tolstoy, Longfellow, Keats, Whittier and Emerson (not every work of each)

✓112. Become familiar with the compositions of Bach, Beethoven, Debussy, Ibert, Mendelssohn, Lalo, Rimsky-Korsakov, Respighi, Liszt, Rachmaninoff, Stravinsky, Toch, Tchaikovsky, Verdi

✓113. Become proficient in the use of a plane, motorcycle, tractor, surfboard, rifle, pistol, canoe, microscope, football, basketball, bow and arrow, lariat and boomerang

✓114. Compose music

✓115. Play *Clair de Lune* on the piano

✓116. Watch fire-walking ceremony (in Bali and Surinam)

✓117. Milk a poisonous snake (bitten by a diamondback rattlesnake during a photo session)

✓118. Light a match with a .22 rifle

✓119. Visit a movie studio

✓120. Climb Great Pyramid of Cheops (Egypt)

✓121. Become a member of the Explorers' Club and the Adventurers' Club

✓122. Learn to play polo

✓123. Travel through the Grand Canyon on foot and by boat

✓124. Circumnavigate the globe (four times)

125. Visit the moon ("someday, if God wills")

✓126. Marry and have children (have two sons and four daughters)

✓127. Live to see the 21st century

(For an extended list of goals, turn to Appendix A.)

During my career as an explorer, I have faced numerous brushes with death, including being charged by an elephant, surviving a plane crash and being attacked by *fellahin*. When I explained my plans to explore the length of the Nile in a kayak, naysayers told me it was "suicidal"—that it had never been done before.

During television and press interviews, one of the commonly asked questions has been, "How many close calls have you had, John?" My usual response was "Several!" When asked for details, I have generally described one or two of my most recent ones. It had never occurred to me to keep track of any of the dangerous predicaments I have faced during my life. After all, these were traumatic experiences and painful to remember. But one writer from the *National Enquirer* requested a list of my most dangerous ordeals. Not having the haziest idea of how many there had been, but curious as to what the actual number was, I began recording the ones I could recall.

The first effort produced a list of twenty, which triggered, over the following days, the remembrance of an additional eighteen. Finally, four more were retrieved from my memory bank, for a surprisingly high total of forty-two near-death experiences, many of which are described in this book.

Some of these escapades were, admittedly, my own fault, due to lapses of sound judgment and sheer recklessness. But others were beyond my control. Except for a critically small difference in time and distance, in several instances of a few feet here or a few seconds there, any one of them could have resulted in my death.

Not included in the forty-two count were dozens of other mini-narrow escapes, since each one lasted only a brief time, and then was over and done with. Also not incorporated in the list were the numerous potentially deadly, actual and "almost-happened" accidents I have experienced during my lifetime while driving various vehicles, from trucks to Jeeps, Land Rovers and sports cars, more than 1 million national and international miles.

Writing an account of each episode proved to be cathartic—releasing strong emotions that were repressed during each crisis and then forgotten soon after. Memories have come flooding back of details not thought about since the original event, confirming that the subconscious *is* truly the storehouse for the memories of all our experiences in life.

Every escape from the Angel of Death has been followed by an intoxicating relief over the miracle of surviving—of being able to continue possessing the gift of life. With each deliverance, there has been a burst of renewed appreciation for the most meaningful sources of happiness—health, family and friends, the infinite beauties and creations of the natural world, the everlasting pleasure of music. I have always valued these blessings, but never more so than after being confronted with certain extinction only to be granted a merciful reprieve. This has never failed to fill me with an even deeper gratitude for being able to continue enjoying each one of them.

There was one episode that proved to be as endangering to my life as any of the others. It also was not counted among those in the list of forty-two, or included in this book, because it was a totally different kind of adventure from the others, and, in a special way, the ultimate survival.

It began in 1983 when a routine physical examination and a subsequent biopsy revealed that I was afflicted with prostate cancer, which had spread to other areas of my body. The grim prognosis was that I had only a 10 percent chance of living five more years. What a blow!

I was thunderstruck. How could this be?!? I had been feeling perfectly well, with no symptoms suggesting any physical problems, and up to now, able to carry out the usual heavy schedule of family activities, coast-to-coast lecturing and overseas travel. A dozen questions raced through my mind—*Surely the prognosis is too pessimistic! Shouldn't I get a second opinion? Isn't there a possibility of a mistake?*

The forecast of having one chance in ten of living only five more years made death seem incredibly close. And what quality of life would I have during the time before the end? Five *full* years wasn't nearly enough time to carry out all of the future plans my wife, Carol, and I had set for ourselves, particularly those involving activities and trips with our four wonderful daughters and two sons. I needed at least another twenty-five years of living to enjoy my family, help grandchildren grow to maturity and achieve at least fifty more life goals.

Hearing the news that I had cancer, with "distant metastasis," hit me with a heavy emotional impact that cast me into a pit of despair. At first I was so depressed that I wanted only to be alone—to retreat to "my cave" and sort things out. But surrounded by caring family and friends I soon abandoned any need for isolation.

I had always been able to cope reasonably well with dozens of life-threatening crises in the past, but all of them had originated from *external* sources, with the exception of the five tropical sicknesses picked up during the Nile expedition: malaria, amoebic dysentery, schistosomiasis, a staphylococcic infection and a pork tapeworm.

But cancer is internal and inaccessible, an invisible menace that can't be defended against directly.

In the politically correct language of our times, I had become "existence challenged," with my longevity now drastically reduced and my demise accelerated. As with previous brushes with death I was faced with two choices. One, I could surrender to the inevitable and accept a foreshortened life with meek resignation, or two, I could choose to ignore the prognosis and take an active role in doing everything possible to fight the disease and survive for many more years.

I recalled the numerous pessimists who, over the years, had tried to discourage me from attempting difficult projects. With little variation, each person always had the same advice: "You'll never be able to do it. It's quite impossible you know!"

If I had listened to them and abandoned my plans, I would have missed out on many of the greatest experiences of my life. But I was always able to forge ahead and achieve success with even the most formidable goals. So there was never any question which choice I would make.

As a result of a therapeutic combination of a strong motivation to live far longer than five years; an inspirational support system, consisting of my devoted wife, family and close friends; and the treatment of an exceptional oncologist, Dr. Gary Lieskovsky at the University of Southern California's Norris Cancer Center in Los Angeles, I have been able to beat the odds again and survive the harsh prognosis. Through Dr. Lieskovsky's skillful surgery and his supervision of the necessary regimen of radiation and chemotherapy, my cancers were either obliterated or have gone into remission. This has enabled me to continue leading an active life, long past the original forecast, right up to the present time.

In addition to the excellent professional care received at the Norris Cancer Center, there were several actions I personally took that, according to Dr. Lieskovsky and others, made a significant contribution toward my recovery. I mention them here in the hopes they might be helpful to others facing a major physical challenge:

1. Upon being informed of the seriousness of my condition, I immediately set the goal of overcoming the disease and regaining normal health.
2. I resolved *never to give up* on reaching this goal. The actions that were crucial to my surviving several of the brushes with death detailed in this book

were also important in helping me attain this goal: the refusal to surrender to "the inevitable," overcoming fear and enduring pain through mental discipline, remaining calm and under control at all times, being optimistic through all circumstances.

3. From personal experience I knew how powerful the mind can be in influencing the body, both for healing or in harming, therefore I promised myself to reject any inclination towards self-pity, depression or bitterness, but instead fill my mind with positive expectations of ultimate success.

4. I began reading books written by individuals who had survived terminal cancer, to find out why and how they had escaped death. Also, I set up a filing system and began filling it with research material, gleaned from library visits, magazine and newspaper articles, dealing with cancer and the various procedures used to treat it.

As I progressed through the surgeries, the long courses of radiation and chemotherapy, the knowledge gained from these studies, together with the information given in response to the questions I asked of Dr. Lieskovsky and the lab technicians, gave me a much clearer understanding of my disease and the treatments I was enduring. This created a feeling of being more an active participant in my healing, rather than just a submissive patient who does nothing more than show up on time for each hospital appointment. Through being better informed I had greater confidence in being able to contribute to the effectiveness of each of my treatments by conjuring up a distinct visualization, during each session, of the destruction of the malignant tumors from the concentrated beams of radiation and the toxic chemicals used in the chemotherapies. The mind-body relationship never felt stronger!

5. Refusing to allow the disease to dominate any area of my life, I began getting back to a regular work schedule soon after completing the professional medical treatments. During the interminable journey down the Nile I discovered how extraordinarily tough the body can be when pushed to the limits of endurance and extreme hardship.

6. Several times during the trip I was able to function adequately in order to fulfill a need, in spite of being desperately weak from sickness and lack of food. This includes, for example, occasions when, after a debilitating malaria attack, I wanted nothing more than to remain in my sleeping bag and rest all day. Always resisting this temptation, I would get back on the river, struggling at first to make any headway, but feeling stronger with each passing hour, so that by nightfall I had paddled twenty or more miles downstream. Through the years since the various procedures I have often repeated this same pattern. There have been many days when I have felt too ill to leave home, but the obligation to fulfill prearranged lecture

and business commitments always gets me back into action. This results in my body becoming energized, blood being oxygenated and my immune system being strengthened, and I end up physically more vigorous. Staying home, particularly in bed every time I feel sick, results in an inward focus with too much awareness of symptoms. While getting back to work there is a healthier concentration of mind and emotion *outward.*

First Adventure
(And Almost the Last)

One of my earliest childhood memories, reinforced by my mother in later years, was an incident I experienced when I was five years old. We were living in Oakland at the time, and I can still remember my excitement when we boarded the ferry to cross the vast, gleaming bay for a day of shopping in San Francisco. The raucous seagulls swooping and wheeling all around us, the scuttling green crabs on the rocks, the colorful starfish clinging to the dock pilings—all were fascinating to me. According to my parents, from the time I could first walk I displayed an insatiable curiosity and interest in nature and all living creatures, from spiders to horses. I frequently had to be restrained from picking up potentially harmful insects or from petting strange animals. (My father once commented, "John is a natural naturalist.")

I had never been on a boat before, and the cruise across the bay was the most thrilling event of my life. I wanted to explore every area of the ferry, from the wheelhouse to the engine room, dragging my long-suffering mother along behind me.

We finally settled down on one of the wooden benches provided for the passengers on the top deck, so that Mom could collapse for a rest. I couldn't sit still for very long, however and, under her vigilant watch, I skipped over to the rail to look down at the beautiful waves churned up by the prow as it cut through the water.

Suddenly, there appeared what to me were large gray fish (actually dolphins), swiftly swimming and diving in the frothy bow waves. What were these incredible creatures that could slice through the water as fast as our boat and not be run over? I was so excited by this mysterious spectacle that I quickly climbed *over the rail* on the ocean side, holding on with both hands, and leaned out for a better view of the graceful creatures. Suppressing a scream, my mother leaped up from the bench and raced over to the rail. With the help of a passenger, she wrenched me back to safety and delivered the scolding of my life.

Years later my mother described this event as one of the most frightening experiences she had been through with me. "I was sure you were going to lose your hold on the rail, fall into the water and drown before we could stop the ferry and rescue you."

Endangered by a Mother's Love

My earliest escape from death occurred one summer when I was ten years old. My parents took me on a camping trip through California, in our four-door blue Buick. With us was my "pal," my little white terrier, Toby—ten pounds of curiosity, fearlessness and loyalty, and my constant companion. It was a great adventure for me each time we camped out in various wilderness areas. After we had unloaded the car, I would help pitch our large green canvas tent and lay our sleeping bags inside. Once we got settled, my folks would relax and read in their folding chairs. Toby and I would take off on a hike in the surrounding forest, with my dog running along ahead of me, his nose close to the ground, excited by the exotic smells he detected.

One of our major destinations on this trip was majestic Sequoia National Park. Upon arriving there, a brief pause at the entrance brought an admonition from the ranger on duty to keep Toby on a leash and provided directions to my father that had us driving down a two-lane dirt road, winding through a magnificent forest of towering sequoias, commonly known as redwoods. I was completely awed by the enormous trees around us. I had never seen anything to compare with them.

As we drove slowly down the road, Toby stood on my lap, paws on the windowsill—tail wagging nonstop. I was aware of how much dogs love trees, and given the size of the sequoias all around us, it must have seemed like Dog Paradise for Toby! Our first stop was at one of the world's most famous trees and, at thirty-five hundred years of age, one of the oldest living things. This was the gigantic sequoia known as the General Sherman. As my father pulled off the road to park, I turned to get Toby's leash. Suddenly he became very excited. He had picked up the scent of something that proved so irresistible that he lunged out of my grip, sailed out the window and raced off toward the great tree at top speed, despite my commands to stop.

Remembering the ranger's warning that dogs were not allowed to run loose in the park, I grabbed the leash and bolted from the car in a dead run after him.

As I neared Toby, I realized his frantic barking was higher in pitch and more intense than I had ever heard before. Seconds later I found out why. Toby had cornered a full-grown doe deer. He was dancing wildly around her, barking hysterically and dashing in repeatedly to nip at her legs.

My little dog was having the most fun of his life, but the doe was furious. She kept turning to face him trying to aim a kick at the harassing dog, who nimbly dodged just out of reach of her lethal pointed hoofs.

Even this close, Toby was too absorbed in the game to obey my commands to come to me. I waited for an opening, grabbing at him several times before I could get a grip on his body. Pulling him to my chest I backed away, but the deer was too enraged to allow me to simply retreat. She attacked. Marching stiff-legged towards us, she reared up and plunged down on me with her front legs, her sharp hoofs striking me on the forehead, gashing it to the bone. Dazed, I fell over backwards. I had been shielding Toby in my arms, but as I fell I was able to push him free. The doe pressed the attack, rearing high again and jabbing me heavily on the chest with both hoofs. I was sure she was going to kill me. When she moved to strike again, Toby came to my rescue. Snapping at the doe's feet, he dashed in close and then retreated quickly so as not to be trampled.

Distracted, the doe moved toward Toby as I scrambled to my feet. Barking furiously, the little dog frisked around her, continuously positioning himself between the deer and me. I snatched him up and ran to the car as fast as I could. The doe aggressively trotted after us, not stopping until I jumped in the car and slammed the door.

My parents had been sitting in the car reading park brochures, unaware of the drama that had unfolded within fifty feet of them. They were shocked to see their son bleeding profusely from a head wound, a battle souvenir from saving his dog, who had immediately returned the favor.

While my upset mother examined my lacerated forehead and bruised chest, I explained the details of the assault in a rush of words. Meanwhile, the doe paced nervously near the car ready to attack again. "Let's get out of here," said Dad, "before that deer breaks a window."

As my father pulled away to drive me to the park's first aid station, I caught sight of two lovely twin fawns standing in the bushes near the General Sherman tree. Obviously, they were awaiting their mother's return. My pain and fright quickly subsided. I was suddenly filled with admiration for the doe and her fearless defense of her fawns. I was also proud of my plucky little defender, Toby, who had very possibly saved me from a fatal goring.

LIFE GOALS #78 & #79: *Free Dive to Forty Feet and Catch a Ten-Inch Abalone*

Nearly Entombed in a Sea Cave

Throughout my life I have loved water in all its forms with an unwavering passion: rivers and streams, lakes and ponds and oceans—any ocean. I have enjoyed each one in every way possible, both above and below the surface, including free diving, body and board surfing, water skiing, fly fishing, deep-sea fishing, ice skating, Jet Skiing, scuba diving, sailing; traveling by hand-paddled canoe and dugout, reed raft and paddle-wheel steamboat; paddling a sixteen foot kayak down the length of the world's longest river, the forty-two hundred mile Nile; shipping aboard a U.S. Merchant Marine freighter as an ordinary seaman and as a passenger aboard several luxury cruise ships.

Growing up on the coast of Southern California enabled me to get to know and love the ocean. As a little boy my favorite thing was having my parents take me to a local beach where I would spend the day splashing in the shallow surf, building little sand castles and chasing the sea birds along the shore.

But I really began my lifelong intimate relationship with the ocean when I was twelve years old and read a travel book on the South Seas. It described how islanders, wearing only goggles, would make deep dives to bring up large flat oysters and occasionally find beautiful pearls inside. I decided to learn to dive as they did and began to explore the mysterious undersea world that had so intrigued me whenever I visited the beaches.

I bought a pair of rubber swimming goggles at a local sports shop and soon was trying them out one Saturday afternoon at the Santa Monica pier. The round wooden pilings supporting the pier were encrusted with a rich variety of sea life. I was delighted at how well the goggles worked, enabling me to get a close view when I dove down and could see underwater clearly for the first time.

I marveled at the vivid colors of the starfish clinging to each of the massive pilings supporting the pier: red, orange, purple and yellow ones. Also, there were elegant flower-like sea anemones, clusters of black rock oysters and olive-green crabs. The water was clear enough for me to see a school of silvery fish feeding on the ocean floor far below. I tried to dive down to reach them but my ears began hurting so badly from the pressure that I had to return to the surface.

By the time I was thirteen I had developed enough skills in swimming and diving that I was able to swim out to rocky reefs beyond the breakers. There I would dive down ten or fifteen feet, grab a sizable spiny lobster and two or three abalone to provide a delicious Sunday dinner for my family. But never more than just enough for one meal.

The ocean became a great character-builder for me, but also sometimes a harsh and unforgiving taskmaster. On several occasions it almost took my life.

I never tired of exploring the fascinating underwater world along the California coast, from San Diego to Monterey. I even dove during the winter months when the water was bone-chillingly cold, wearing only a flannel sweatshirt and pants to help retain my body heat. I discovered that by entering the frigid water quickly, in a state of total relaxation, my body would grow numb all over, enabling me to swim and dive for as long as forty-five minutes. About that time, I would begin shivering uncontrollably and have to return to the beach and slowly warm up in the sun.

One of my favorite diving areas was the beautiful coastal shore near La Jolla, California. The water was always wonderfully clear and teeming with myriad forms of sea life. One summer afternoon at the age of sixteen, I was swimming underwater at a depth of about ten feet.

Wearing face mask and swim fins and holding my breath about thirty to forty seconds with each dive, I began investigating some of the crevices at the base of the rugged cliff fronting the shoreline. There were red spiny lobsters and gray-green conger eels occupying the larger niches, with grapefruit-sized purple sea urchins carpeting the ocean floor.

As I finned along, weaving through the skeins of kelp anchored to the rocky bottom, I came upon an opening in the face of the cliff and cautiously entered a narrow underwater cave. When my eyes adjusted to the dim, greenish light, I could see a foot-wide shelf extending along the left-hand wall. But what really caught my attention was the sight of a huge abalone, a single shell mollusca at least ten inches across, attached to the ceiling.

I often carried an automobile tire iron with me when diving to pry off abalone; they can adhere to a rock surface with a powerful suction of up to three hundred pounds per square inch. Unfortunately, the bar was back in my equipment bag on shore. On previous dives I had discovered that it was possible to pop an "ab" free with my fingers by catching it by surprise, when it was relaxed and had raised its shell slightly in order to filter out organic food particles from the water.

Eager to collect the big shellfish, I decided to take a chance and try for it using the manual technique. I slowly extended my flattened hands into the niche, careful not to alarm the abalone. But just as I was about to pounce and dislodge it, a sudden surge of tidal current swept into the cave knocking me off balance.

With nothing else to hold on to, and in imminent danger of being painfully scraped along the jagged barnacle-encrusted wall next to me, I unthinkingly grabbed and held on to the nearest edge of the abalone's shell. The startled creature instantly clamped down hard on the first joints of my fingers of both hands, trapping me tightly in its vise-like grip.

I had read of several tragedies in which free divers had been trapped and drowned by abalone, including that of a California lifeguard. The husky athlete had disappeared one morning from his observation platform. After extensive searching, his friends finally located his body on the ocean floor just offshore, with one hand still trapped under a large abalone.

In a panic, I fought to escape and managed to wrench my left hand free, but three fingers of my right hand were still firmly trapped under the heavy shell. As I struggled my fingers became lacerated by the rough edges, oozing blood that resembled tendrils of green smoke.

By now I was desperate for air but realized my only chance for survival was to calm down and remain perfectly still. After an interminable time I felt the abalone relax and ease off the pressure. It was just enough for me to jerk my hand free and make a dash back to the surface.

As I plunged down to the entrance of the grotto my escape was blocked for a dangerous few seconds by a thick plug of seaweed carried part way into the opening by the surging tide. By the time I had clawed my way through the barrier all the air in my lungs was used up. I had been underwater for at least three minutes—longer than ever before in my life. As I shot to the sunlit surface I could no longer hold my breath and, with an explosive gasp, released my control, sucking in as much water as air.

I collapsed on a cliffside ledge above the ocean, totally

exhausted and dizzy from the near drowning.

I lay without moving for most of an hour, soaking up the warmth of the late afternoon sun, and gradually regained my strength. I had been humbled by the harrowing experience and felt grateful in having lived through it in such good condition, except for the raw gashes on my fingers.

But the challenge of the giant abalone was just too big a temptation to resist, and with my usual high energy level back to normal, I resolved to bring it up as a wonderful addition to my shell collection.

I dove back down to the cave, this time with my long tire iron in hand, and managed to pry free the splendid trophy—the biggest and most dangerous abalone I was ever to capture.

Surf's Up—Too High!

When I was seventeen, I had another ocean adventure that nearly resulted in my being drowned. Two of my high school buddies, George and Loren, joined me to go body surfing at Malibu Beach, California, one Saturday in December.

I began this exciting sport when I was thirteen, before learning to ride the waves on a surfboard. Catching a wave at just the right moment as it breaks and with the body shaped in just the right position results in a really marvelous rush toward shore, the momentum of the wave sweeping you in all the way to the sand. We arrived at the beach on a chilly, overcast afternoon. We spread a blanket and sat in awe watching a succession of giant breakers rushing toward us. We had heard radio reports about how a violent storm far out at sea had been causing unusually high and destructive surf activity along the coast. Each wave would build up in height as it reached the shallows, crest in a slow curl, then crash down in a frothy explosion that sounded like an earthshaking thunderclap. Driven by gale force winds for hundreds of miles over the open sea and unimpeded by any land mass, the combers were the biggest and roughest we had ever seen.

After a brief discussion we decided that, since we were strong swimmers and experienced body surfers, it would be exciting to challenge the waves. Brashly overconfident, we put on our swim trunks and sweat shirts and dove into the cold, foamy ocean. We came up gasping from the shock of the icy water on our warm bodies. We spread out and began swimming toward the towering swells, some of them reaching a height of ten feet as they crested.

As we swam out I felt an electrifying thrill run through me, similar to the feeling of charging down a field with my football team toward the opposing players. In this case the monster storm waves were our menacing opponents, powerful and dangerous.

The first wave broke in front of me, plunging down with fearsome power. I dove for the bottom so that the main turbulence swept above my body. There was a succession of waves followed by a calm period, which gave my friends and me ample time to get in position and prepare for our first ride to shore.

With careful timing I caught a massive oncoming breaker just after it had curled over and began its swooping descent. I hunched my upper body to create a better surface for the rushing water. It was exhilarating beyond description! George and Loren had great runs also, and they joined me in bellowing out war whoops as we headed out for another turn.

The next two rides were just as exciting but really scary, the waves so violent that I felt out of control with each one. I decided to settle for one final trip and then call it a day. I should have quit while I was ahead.

There was no problem swimming back to the breakers, but when attempting to catch the next wave I was off in my timing. I found myself at the top of the giant breaker with a momentary heart-stopping glimpse of the churning flood far below. With a loud explosion the wave, with me inside it, crashed down in a foaming avalanche that smashed me into the pebbly ocean floor. My arms and legs were gashed in a dozen places as I was helplessly swept along end over end along the abrasive bottom. It was like being in a giant cement mixer, with the violent current battering me in its deadly grip. I felt as though I was going to die at any moment.

Completely disoriented, I had no idea where the surface was and I was frantic for air. When I finally found it, there was only enough time for me to snatch one breath. Then the second wave hit. I was sucked down and again raked over the ocean floor, my chest and back getting scratched deep enough to draw blood.

Reaching shallow water I was able to raise my head above the surface and gulp in deep breaths of air. Though carried right up to the edge of the sandy shore, I was too weak to do anything but get to my knees and cough up some of the water I had swallowed. With blood oozing from numerous small wounds I finally was able to stagger over to George and Loren resting on the blanket. Sensibly, they had returned to the beach after their second ride in the pounding waves.

After landing, they had spotted me out in the midst of the breakers, seemingly having a good time and in no difficulty. From past shared experiences in skin-diving, hiking and rock climbing, they had developed confidence in my ability to cope with dangerous situations. In this case their confidence was totally unjustified.

"Goddard, you look like something the cat drug in!" said George. "No, more like a wounded zombie," said Loren. After hearing what had happened, they agreed I was extremely lucky to have survived the ordeal. My gashes healed within a week but the memory of the terrifying, near-death experience never left me, and periodic nightmares kept it fresh in my mind. But I learned a major lesson in common sense, and never again did I surf waves beyond my ability to handle them.

LIFE GOAL #130: *Explore Catalina Island*

Catalina Cliff-Hanger

Santa Catalina Island, twenty-four miles off the Southern California coast, has always been one of my favorite places to visit. The most unforgettable visit came one summer when I was seventeen and had just graduated from Los Angeles High School. A pal, Joe Anderson, and I spent a week camping out on a chaparral-covered hillside above Avalon, the only town on the twenty mile-long island.

We found a perfect campsite under a small oak tree with leafy branches that spread out in all directions, forming an ideal shelter. Shrubs and grasses growing around the young tree completely hid us from view when we were in our sleeping bags inside. We could see out, but not be seen.

Joe and I had kitchen and bathroom privileges with our friends, the Gibby family. They had rented an apartment just a few minutes' hike from our camp. Each morning, while Joe spent time with the Gibbys, I would walk down to the port area and wait for the Catalina Ferry to sail in from Wilmington on the mainland. As the big boat maneuvered in to tie up at the dock, the passengers would line the rail and throw coins, usually quarters and dimes, down to several of us teenagers swimming in the sparkling clear water next to the ferry, in friendly competition for the money. In a burst of enthusiastic generosity, one lady tossed down a dollar bill. It fluttered along erratically in the breeze, finally landing next to one of the divers who snatched it up with a smile and a wave of appreciation. Once a coin was retrieved, we would cram it into our mouths until we looked like chipmunks with bulging cheeks.

When the ferry departed for the return to the coast and the other boys had swum back to shore, I would dive down twenty-five or thirty feet to scavenge the bottom of the marina for the coins that had been missed. I was able to get down deeper and stay down longer than most of the other divers since water sports were my favorite recreation and had been great for developing my stamina and endurance. Usually I would collect five or six dollars worth of coins to help pay for my daily expenses.

After stashing the dive money at the Gibbys', I would return to the ocean and revel in the pleasure of exploring the luxuriant jungles of kelp and the rocky reefs with their prolific sea life just offshore. As I snorkeled along, I watched one little drama unfold as a two-foot octopus emerged from a hidey-hole between the boulders on the bottom and went blooping along in a series of spasmodic movements that attracted a large, dark green conger eel from his shelter. The eel darted forward and with its needle-sharp teeth nipped off a tentacle from the unwary octopus, which immediately released a protective inky cloud to hide in. After the eel had devoured the sucker-studded tentacle, he sinuously swam back to his victim and was about to bite off another arm when I decided to intervene. I dove down and shooed away the attacker and watched as the little octopus scooted safely out of the eel's territory. Later, I surprised two large black bat rays cruising over the ocean floor. Upon seeing me, they accelerated in an amazing burst of speed, then flashed over my head like a pair of jet fighters and were gone.

One hot afternoon, Joe and I, accompanied by the Gibbys' son, Reed, set off up the mountain towering above Avalon on a day-long nature hike. We were headed for the beach eight miles away on the other side of Catalina, following wildlife trails and fire-breaks. Along the way we encountered a covey of quail, a small rattlesnake, several deer and wild goats, and even a charming little island fox.

When we breathlessly reached the crest of the mountain, there were spectacular panoramas of the rugged island and the Pacific Ocean on both sides of us. To the east we could clearly see the coast of Southern California and to the west an endless sweep of dark blue sea extending to the far horizon.

We continued down a trail leading to the beach far below, at the base of steep, high cliffs, to enjoy a swim and some rest before heading back to Avalon. As we descended single-file over the narrow trail, I spotted a full-grown black goat kneeling to drink at a pool on a ledge below the trail. Joe and Reed waited while I quietly crept down until I was only a few yards above the billy goat, who was so intent on drinking that he hadn't detected me as yet.

Acting on a sudden impulse I jumped up, slid down the side of the ledge, made a leap of eight or nine feet to the edge of the pool and grabbed the goat by one horn and its tail just as it stood up to flee. The ram, caught completely off-guard, bleated loudly in fright and struggled to escape.

"Come and see my new friend," I called to Joe and Reed.

"Okay, John, what are you going to do with him now?" asked Joe.

"First I'm going to convince him that I really am a friend, then let him go," I said.

For several minutes, I sat next to the frightened animal stroking him and speaking soothing words until he ceased his exertions and began to relax. When the goat seemed reassured that I wasn't a threat or going to harm him, I released my hold and was pleased to have him move off placidly with no further sign of fear.

When I tried to climb back to the trail it dawned on me that I was in serious trouble. In scrambling down to the ledge, my vigorous movements had caused a rockslide that had effectively sheared off any footholds or handholds that would have enabled me to return to my friends above.

I checked to see where the billy goat had gone, but couldn't see him anywhere. It appeared that he had followed a crack extending along the cliff face where only a sure-footed goat could travel and then climbed to the footpath and had gone on from there.

We hadn't brought a rope with us, so there was no way Joe and Reed could pull me up to them. Even when Joe held Reed's legs and lowered him toward me I still couldn't reach his hands, and even if I could have, my 170-pound weight and the sharp rocks would have frustrated that attempt. I was trapped on the ledge with nowhere to go but down the steep face of the cliff three hundred feet to the rocky beach below.

"Meet me down at the beach, guys, I'm going to do a little rock-climbing," I said, attempting to sound more confident than I felt.

My friends moved down the trail as I cautiously stepped to the edge of the cliff and was shocked to see how precipitous it was. I lay chest-down, swung my legs over the cliff top and began slowly working my way downwards.

On excursions to various rocky areas of California's Mojave Desert and in the canyons of Utah, I had developed some experience in climbing steep cliffs. However, never had I tackled a cliff face so nearly vertical and so difficult as this one. It consisted of shale, the most treacherous and unstable rock to climb on. It was created in ancient times by deposits of clay, mud and sand, compacted into dense layers that separate and crumble when stressed too much.

Clinging unsteadily to the rock wall I was forced to press the front of my body as flat against the surface as possible. This drastically limited my view of conditions below me to just a few yards so that I had no idea of the best descent to follow.

As I crept downward, foot by foot, I probed nervously with fingers and feet for the slightest crack or knob of rock that could provide some support that would keep me from falling. Just as one foot- or hand-hold would crumble, I was able to slide down and dig into another nubbin as I tumbled down. Several times I was only able to stop my descent by holding onto a small projection with just one hand while my feet thrashed around desperately trying to find an edge to settle on. I kept up an incessant mantra of *Stay calm! Stay calm! Stay calm! You're going to make it!*

Less than halfway down I became conscious of faint shouts that I couldn't understand. I turned my head just enough to look seaward and saw a fishing boat offshore with people lining the rail, shouting and waving. Then I realized they were trying to tell me, "Go back! Go back!" Someone with a searchlight aimed it my way and began blinking out a message in Morse code, but in my precarious position I was too frazzled and endangered to interpret it.

In feeling my way over a hump on the cliff I suddenly lost my footing and slid several heart-stopping feet before being able to dig in and come to a halt. My legs turned to rubber and I began trembling all over as I realized how close I had come to falling onto the boulders one hundred feet below. As I had been clawing at the rock surface desperately seeking any kind of depression to arrest my slide, the fingernail on the index finger of my left hand was violently ripped nearly off when it caught on a sharp edge. I yelped in pain.

It hurt terribly, but my entire focus was on getting down alive. This was just the worst of the bruises and gashes I had acquired during what seemed like a continuous fall in extreme slow motion.

There were other scary moments of slipping, made especially painful by my lacerated fingers and detached fingernail. I sweated from fear and the blazing sun, but finally I was able to jump down the last few feet onto a patch of soft sand and find a large, flat rock to recuperate on. I collapsed on top of it with a huge sigh of relief and then became aware of the sound of applause emanating from the fishing boat still anchored offshore—a touching accolade for the audacious "human fly" and his miraculous survival.

Joe and Reed found me half-asleep on the warm rock a few minutes later. When they looked up at the cliff it appeared so sheer and so devoid of any possible way down that at first they accused me of finding another route to descend on and reach the beach. They became convinced, however, when they looked at my torn and filthy clothing and my fingers and hands, the bloody evidence of the most difficult climb of my life. From the base, the awesome palisade towering above us looked impossible even to me!

A Near Miss at Scott Air Force Base

A close encounter with death while stationed at Scott Air Force Base in Belleville, Illinois, gives a grim example of how a sudden change of mind or alteration of plans can sometimes mean the difference between living or dying.

During my six-week assignment at the base I make friends with one of the air force pilots also stationed there, Captain Frank Cunningham. One of his duties is to fly a final test of aircraft that have been serviced or repaired by the maintenance mechanics.

On one flight I am with him in a little two-passenger L-4 "Grasshopper," used only for observation purposes. This is the smallest, lightest and slowest plane in the air force, so light and low-powered in fact that pilots, flying the L-4 into unexpected headwinds, suddenly find themselves moving at zero miles per hour and even being blown backwards!

We are creeping along at the painfully slow cruising speed of seventy miles per hour when the engine begins coughing and missing. This is alarming since we are flying over a suburb of St. Louis at a low altitude of five hundred feet, with no emergency landing area in sight.

We spot one open space in the sea of homes below, but it is a school football field with students everywhere. As we begin losing speed and altitude, Frank noses the plane down in a shallow dive to avoid stalling out and, with no place to set down, heads for the broad Mississippi River ahead of us.

The slow landing speed and the light weight of the plane give us a good chance of surviving a ditching in the river. We just have to avoid the barge traffic, get out of the plane fast and swim to shore.

There is ample fuel remaining, so running out is not the source of the trouble, but in checking over the instruments Frank discovers that the carburetor heat control has been installed backwards and though it appears in the "off" position it actually has been fully "on" ever since takeoff. This causes the engine to seize up and begin choking out. Frank quickly shuts off the valve, the engine revives and we head back to the base with no further trouble.

The most exciting air adventure with Frank comes when I fly with him in an SB2C "Helldiver." During a power dive, Frank pushes the plane one hundred miles per hour faster than its "red line" speed, the maximum recommended operational speed of the Helldiver. When we pull out of the dive the plane shudders and creaks from the heavy strain of the high G-force.

Suddenly, we hear a staccato burst of sound as an entire row of rivets pops out of a seam on top of the right wing. Frank eases up on the stick, slowly levels the plane and, flying with a light touch to minimize any further strain on the damaged wing, returns to base for a safe landing.

One day Frank phones to invite me to go with him, a copilot and an engineer on an afternoon test flight in a twin-engine bomber trainer. I am about to accept, but I tell him I first have to clear my appointment schedule.

A notice has been posted on our bulletin board announcing a special lecture for all personnel in my sector. It is scheduled for just after lunch in the base theatre.

Though greatly tempted to skip the program and go on the far more appealing flight, I decide, having missed the previous lecture, to do the responsible thing and attend this one instead.

This decision proves to be fateful—a critical matter of life or death. When I come out of the auditorium the base is abuzz with the news that a Scott-based aircraft has crashed and burned.

As details are revealed I am shocked to hear that Frank's aircraft has been lost. Evidently, a fuel line on the trainer ruptured. This resulted in gas leaking out, accumulating in one of the wings and then, only twenty minutes after takeoff, exploding, instantly killing Frank and his two companions in the ensuing fireball.

If I had not made the decision to attend the lecture I would have been aboard the plane at the time it blew up, and I would have been killed along with my friend and the two other men.

LIFE GOAL #265: *Become a Certified Scuba Diver*

Trapped in an Undersea Jungle

O ne of the most vivid memories of my early teens was the day I discovered the magnificent undersea fairyland of a vast kelp forest. A friend of mine and I swam out from the beach, towing an inflated inner tube as a float to rest on between dives.

We would dive to increasing depths as our ears adjusted to the pressure. It was exhilarating wandering for hours through the jungle of golden kelp, zigzagging between the giant fronds that soared upwards thirty feet from rocky holdfasts on the ocean floor to the sun-drenched surface.

There was an unending procession of sea life around us—leopard and horned sharks; graceful bat rays; bright orange Garibaldi perch; calico bass; red, black and white sheepshead fish; mackerel and many more. On the sandy bottom, lying in wait for prey and perfectly camouflaged under a thin layer of sand, were stingrays, halibut and shovelnosed sharks.

I was startled when a sea lion flashed past me in a swirl of bubbles, then returned to look me over. The sea lion was so surprised at encountering such a strange creature as me twenty feet underwater that it defecated as it performed a perfect circle around me, so that I was encircled by a ring of powdery dung.

Years later, I am enjoying recreational diving in this same kelp bed, this time wearing a scuba outfit, when I come dangerously close to having a fatal accident.

After being underwater for forty-five minutes, I run out of air in my single tank. By pulling an emergency lever, an additional three minutes of air becomes available, enough for me to investigate a harmless angel shark resting on the sand nearby.

I stealthily approach from the rear of the shark and, thinking I might get a free tow, grab its tail. The surprised fish shoots forward at full speed and with such tremendous force that my face mask and one of my fins are swept off. After recovering them, I look around to see where the shark has gone and spot it only one hundred feet away, again lying quietly on the sandy bottom. Better prepared this time, I come up behind it, grab its tail with all my strength and, holding my mask on with one hand, have a fun ride as the shark tows me through the water as fast as it can travel.

As it slows down, I release it and then become aware that my reserve air is almost exhausted. It is getting difficult to breathe through the mouthpiece of my demand regulator. I promptly head for the surface forty feet above. The floating seaweed on top forms such a thick mat that it is difficult to see any thin spot where I can break through.

I swim along a few feet under the seemingly impenetrable brown canopy, becoming increasingly anxious as my air runs out. There seems to be no opening for me to escape through. When I first began diving in the kelp area there were numerous breaks in the mass floating on the surface. However, while I was moving along over the ocean floor, tidal swells had compacted the seaweed, closing off any sizeable gap. Finally, a shimmering shaft of sunlight slanting down through the kelp appears like a providential beacon of hope. With great relief, I rush toward it, ready to charge through the hole and reach the fresh air above.

But just as I shoot upwards a double strand of kelp becomes lodged between the base of my neck and the valve unit on top of my scuba tank, like a predatory tentacle stopping me abruptly.

With no tank air left and barely able to hold my breath much longer, I frantically reach back with both hands to tear the kelp off, but I can't budge it.

Then I push downwards, attempting to break free that way, but the cable of seaweed is so firmly stuck that it still restrains me as if I have been lassoed with a heavy lariat. It seems absurd that only a few inches away from my upturned face is the open air and safety, yet I can't escape to it. My next thought is to pull my knife from its scabbard to cut myself free. At that moment, I can't hold my breath any longer, so there is no time left to do anything but release my harness straps and jettison my leaded weight belt and tank. As they sink to the bottom, I lunge upward through the opening in the kelp and fill my lungs with delicious pure air. I am safe!

LIFE GOALS #15 & #159: *Study Tribal Cultures in Kenya and Visit Mombasa and Fort Jesus*

Kenya Smash-Up

he most arduous ocean voyage I have ever experienced occurred when I traveled aboard the twenty-thousand-ton French passenger liner, *Champollion,* from Marseilles, France, to Mombasa, Kenya. . . .

There are four hundred French passengers, a few other Europeans and me, the only American.

I am heading for Kenya to begin a project to study and film various tribes in East Africa and have chosen to travel by ship to fulfill a boyhood goal of passing through the Suez Canal.

After crossing the Mediterranean, we pause at Port Said to pick up an Egyptian pilot to take over the helm and steer us through the one-hundred-mile-long canal. We are last in a convoy of six ships. A freak accident occurs as we pass a newly constructed but uncompleted canal on our starboard side.

During their passage, the bow waves of the ships ahead of us cause a breach in a temporary dam of packed sand and force a massive amount of water up the channel. Without warning, a six-foot wall of pent-up water comes surging out and smashes into the aft section of the *Champollion.*

The impact causes our ship to veer dangerously off course. It happens so fast that the Egyptian pilot is helpless to keep us from careening into the right bank. The flood shoves the stern away in the opposite direction. We hear a sickening grinding sound as the ship's screws crunch into the shallower bottom of the canal near the port side. We quickly get back on course, continue on through the canal and anchor for the night in the bay at Suez, Egypt.

The next morning, in an effort to be helpful and with the captain's permission, I put on my diving mask and swim fins and dive thirty feet down to check the damage to the ship's huge propellers. Passengers lining the rail watch curiously as I dive off the lower deck and disappear into the bay. Some become upset when I don't come up after a minute or so, but the dive takes at least two minutes; by the time I break the surface, several are convinced that I have drowned or sharks have gotten me.

After the dive, I return to the bridge and make a sketch for the captain, to show him how two of the three screws have been bent out of alignment by the accident. He appreciates my report, but, understandably, cannot accept it as "official." For insurance purposes it has to be documented by a professional diver.

A Greek diver is contacted on shore and hired for the job. He motors out into the bay in a dilapidated fishing boat and anchors near our ship. The passengers and I line the railings and watch with interest as he struggles into a heavy canvas suit, with lead shoes and belt. With the help of two assistants, a big, round copper "hard hat" is placed over his head and bolted to the metal neck gasket of his suit. While one of his crew cranks air into his outfit, he steps onto a wooden platform and is hoisted up by a small derrick and lowered over the side of the boat into the oily water.

Upon completion of his dive, he presents an official inspection certificate to the captain, verifying that two of the three screws are seriously twisted out of shape from impacting the bottom of the canal. He also submits a bill for five hundred dollars for his three-hour job.

Repairing the propellers in Suez would require an unacceptably long delay, plus the expensive obligation of transporting the passengers to Mombasa by alternate means of transportation. Therefore, the captain decides to sail on, even thought it means shutting down the two damaged screws and limping along at five knots. This is less than one third of our normal cruising speed, down the most stifling, sun-scorched expanse of water on Earth—the twelve-hundred-mile-long Red Sea.

During the endless hours of sailing at our reduced speed, I pass the time on deck with my binoculars and in extensive reading, exercising and playing chess with different passengers. One of my chess partners is Jules Petre, a charming Belgian with movie-star good looks, a mane of dark wavy hair and a Royal Air Force fighter-pilot mustache. He has been on a sabbatical leave to his home city, Brussels. Now he is returning to his assignment as a district commissioner in the little country of Rwanda in central Africa.

During the two weeks of our Red Sea voyage, Jules teaches me a working vocabulary of Swahili and regales me with numerous captivating tales of his experiences in Africa. By the time we dock, five days late, at Mombasa, we have become close friends.

Jules has purchased a beautiful new Chevrolet car in Brussels and plans to drive it back, all the way across Kenya and Uganda, to his headquarters in Rwanda. This part of Africa is completely unknown to me, so when he invites me to accompany him on this adventurous safari, and since I have some uncommitted time before starting my African expedition, I accept enthusiastically.

Jules promises to take me on a tour of some of the villages of the Tutsi, the tallest people in Africa, and of the Hutus, the largest tribe in Rwanda.

During the weekend we spend in Nairobi, Kenya's capital, Jules learns of a farmer who has pedigreed boxer puppies for sale. Since he wants to take a dog back to his home for a pet, he decides to visit the breeder at his farm near Thomsen Falls, 150 miles to the east. We leave at dawn and drive through rolling green hills and dense bush, finally locating the farm by noon. Jules and I are shown several young boxers, and we have no trouble choosing the one that is the most exuberantly energetic and affectionate.

When Jules asks me to name the pup I suggest "Blaze" because of the attractive white pattern on his face. After paying the farmer, we depart with Jules at the wheel and Blaze resting contentedly on my lap.

We drive for a few miles, cruising along over a two-lane dirt road at about forty miles an hour. There has been no traffic in sight all morning in this isolated area, so it was startling to encounter a car approaching us in a cloud of dust as we are rounding a sharp curve. Jules has been driving in the middle of the road to avoid the worst potholes. But now, at the sight of the car bearing down on us, his natural reaction is to swerve over to the right lane, the side he has been driving on in Belgium and in Rwanda, momentarily forgetting that in Kenya, driving is on the left.

The other driver, a white Kenyan, also follows his natural instincts and veers to his left side of the road, heading directly into our path. I shout, "To the left, Jules! To the left!" but it is too late. The two cars crash together, head-on, with a terrific impact and a deafening detonation of breaking metal and glass.

It all happens in a matter of seconds, the sudden surprise of meeting the car in front of us, the eerie silence just before colliding, the paralyzing conflict between reason and reaction—then the electrifying smash-up.

We have been wearing our lap belts but no torso restraints. The explosive force of the collision slams Jules's head and chest violently into the steering wheel, severely cutting and bruising his face and breaking several ribs.

The steering wheel is bent in half from Jules hitting it.

The impact is intensified by the heavy trunks and suit-cases, loaded on the backseat and floor, ramming into our front seats. At the last moment, as I realize we are going to crash, I tighten my grip on Blaze and brace my feet firmly on the upper section of the floor. When we hit, my upper body and knees are smashed into the glove compartment and dashboard with such sledgehammer force that at first I can't move. It feels as though bones in my arms and legs are fractured, and I nearly pass out from the pain. But Blaze snaps me out of my stunned condition when he goes wild with terror from the accident, whimpering and squirming uncontrollably. My arms have been wrapped around his body, shielding him from serious injury, but when I roll down the window to crawl out he leaps off my lap, jumps out the window and races off into the dense underbrush along the road. The front section of our car is destroyed, accordioned to half its size by the thirty-mile-an-hour collision, so that it is impossible to open my door.

Gritting my teeth and moving awkwardly, I manage to squeeze through the door window and lower myself to the ground. Still groggy and barely able to walk, I hobble around the rear of our Chevrolet to check on Jules. He is slumped over, unconscious and moaning with pain, with his bloody head resting on the buckled steering wheel. Then I move over to the other car and find the dazed and bloody-faced driver spitting teeth into his cupped hand.

I offer him profuse apologies for the accident, explaining the confusion of right lane–left lane driving. He is in a state of shock, but after a few minutes, when he is able to speak, he is remarkably gracious and understanding.

After clearing his mouth of the eight teeth he has lost, he introduces himself as Mr. Barnes, a businessman from Nairobi. Then, too weak to sit up, he lies down on the front seat and closes his swollen eyes.

As I return to Jules, I examine the wrecked cars, their radiators mashed together and steaming in the afternoon sun. Oil seeping from the wrecks forms dark pools on the dusty road. I realize just how lucky we are to have survived the accident. It is evident that if either car had been traveling a few miles an hour faster, none of us would be alive.

Jules recovers consciousness and is resting on the seat, completely incapacitated and finding it difficult to speak except to acknowledge my report on the injuries of the other driver.

After a half hour of restless waiting, a car finally comes by and stops. Once the driver understands our situation he is immediately sympathetic. Luckily, he is headed for Nakuru, twenty miles away, and generously agrees to drive Jules and Mr. Barnes directly to the hospital there, and also send back a tow truck.

He helps me get the two injured men into his sedan and then drives off. While I wait for the truck, I take a quick survey of my injuries from the accident and am relieved to find no evidence of broken bones. There is an unusual band of crimson skin across my forehead and a bleeding cut above my right eye. The front of my mouth is also sore and bleeding from my teeth gashing into it during the impact. My arms and legs are the most seriously hurt, with heavy bruises that impair my use of them. I am grateful, though, that I can still function and do not have to be hospitalized. The accident leaves me with a feeling that I am very lucky to have come through the crash in such relatively good condition. After my self-exam, I limp into the bush to search for Blaze, calling out periodically in hopes he will respond. After an hour and still unsuccessful, I return to the road grimly discouraged about him living through the oncoming night in this wilderness where nocturnal predators, such as leopard and hyena, are common and would consider Blaze a rare delicacy.

Just at dusk, the tow truck appears, driven by a genial Kenyan. In a matter of minutes, he pulls the wrecks apart, pushes one of them to the side of the road, attaches the other car to his hoist and has us underway and heading for Nakuru.

Three days after the crash, while I am visiting Jules in his private room, a Kikuyu villager appears at the hospital carrying Blaze in a reed basket slung over his back. A local chief had spread the word at the village closest to the accident site that there was a big reward for anyone who could find the missing pup and deliver him to the hospital where Jules is convalescing.

He had devoted much of his time each day on a search effort and had found Blaze just that morning cowering in the grass next to a stream.

The African had transported the dog all the way to Nakuru on his bicycle and now waited to receive the reward.

Except for still being very nervous, and famished from

lack of food, the dog is in good condition. Considering the brief time that Blaze has been with us, both Jules and I are surprised by his joyous reaction to our reunion. He dances around us excitedly in instant recognition, as if he has always been our pet!

Jules hands his rescuer the reward, a five-pound note, equivalent to two weeks' wages for menial work. The man examines the bill for a moment, then tosses it on the floor. With a Kikuyu nurse acting as interpreter, this mysterious behavior is explained. The villager has never before had occasion to use paper currency, only metal coins. Therefore he feels the bill is useless to him. But I am able to convert the five pounds into one hundred silver shillings at a local shop, put them in a heavy plastic sack and present this more suitable reward to one very delighted and relieved rescuer.

LIFE GOAL #141: *Explore the Kagera River*

Kagera Is Spelled
C-A-T-A-S-T-R-O-P-H-E

f you know anything about the "Queen of Rivers," the magnificent Nile River, you know why the river's million-square-mile basin offers everything that makes Africa so appealing. Its water provides the main source of life for a huge population, representing numerous races, from the fair-skinned to the dark, from pygmies to giants, from pagans to Muslims and Christians. The shores of the river are lined with the world's most spectacular monuments of ancient history. The Nile basin is inhabited by every major species of animal and reptile and the greatest variety of birds in Africa. The Nile's primary source is Lake Victoria, the world's second largest freshwater lake, with an area of

26,700 miles. The largest city in Africa, Cairo, is near the river's mouth.

Ultimately, I came to understand that if the Nile had never existed, the country of Egypt—a desert land defined by the river's water and fertilizing silt—could never have existed either. And without Egypt and its enormous contributions to humanity, the entire course of history would have been significantly altered. Yet, remarkably, the river had never been explored in its entirety by anyone. So this became my unwavering dream: to conduct the first exploration of the great Nile River, from its source in central Africa to its mouth at the Mediterranean Sea.

Accompanied by two French explorers, Jean Laporte and André Davy, I fulfill this goal over a period of nine months, in spite of continual pessimism and a complete lack of encouragement from any source other than a few family members and close friends.

My French companions, both from Paris, are two of the toughest and bravest men I have ever known. They are also polar opposites in temperament, personality and even appearance. Jean is a lean, thirty-one-year-old scholar, with pale blue eyes, blond hair and fair complexion. André is a thirty-six-year-old writer and journalist, short of stature but with an athletic build, dark hair and eyes, and a mischievous sense of humor. At twenty-six, I am five years younger than Jean and ten years younger than André, but our ages have no bearing on our successes or failures during the expedition.

Together, we plan to produce a detailed record of our

daily experiences in going down the Nile. Jean, a talented artist, will document the trip with sketch pad and still camera. Also, he will collect entomological specimens for the French Museum of Natural History.

André will send periodic accounts for worldwide distribution along the way to the prestigious Agence France Presse. I will produce the first complete photographic record of the Nile, shooting a sixteen-millimeter film for television and the lecture platform, and taking still photographs with my thirty-five-millimeter cameras to illustrate my projected book on the expedition.

By using my life savings, combined with a hefty bank loan, I am able to finance the total expenses for the three of us over a period of ten months.

My original plan is to travel down the Nile by means of dugouts on the southern half of the river and then by Arab *felucca* on the northern half. But Jean, with fifteen years of kayaking experience on European rivers, wants to use kayaks for the entire Nile. After a shakedown trip on the Marne and Seine rivers in France, André and I give our enthusiastic approval. The kayaks are quiet, maneuverable and nonpolluting. They are also ideal for enabling us to travel independently and at our own speed.

"A trip down the Nile in those cockleshells?" blurts the chief customs officer as we present our equipment for his inspection upon landing at Mombasa, the main port of Kenya. "You must be crackers!" I have to laugh at his tactless but honest reaction. However, at only sixteen feet in length and sixty pounds in weight, our little Eskimo-type boats do look pathetically inadequate for traveling thousands of miles down the longest river in the world, a journey equivalent to paddling from Los Angeles to Lima, Peru, or from New York to Naples, Italy.

His skepticism is echoed by every government official, every authority and every expert (self-styled or genuine) that we have met and would meet from Paris to central Africa.

"A foolhardy attempt at doing the impossible!" we are told.

"A journey dangerous beyond words!"

"A triple suicide by kayak!"

Not that anyone tries to hinder us. Most officials are generally helpful and hospitable. However, they always feel duty-bound to remind us that we will be facing the same obstacles that have turned back or brought fatal disaster to others who have attempted to trace the entire river: the same dangerous wildlife, trackless swamps, roaring cataracts, deadly diseases, sandstorms, hostile villagers and relentless heat—all still present with undiminished menace.

Of course they are right. Extensive research has forewarned me about these problems. Even several of my friends and relatives are not able to understand why I want to leave the security and comfort of home to embark on such a Herculean undertaking in such a remote part of the world. I try to convince the skeptics that I always derive immense inner rewards, spiritual growth and a deep sense of satisfaction in experiencing the unknown; in encountering rare sights, different cultures and raw adventure; and especially in savoring the enchantments of unspoiled nature. In going down the Nile I will be answering an irresistible siren call I have heard since boyhood—to come to Africa and experience all these attractions in the most profound way possible.

The Nile expedition proves to be, without question, the greatest adventure of an adventure-filled life. It is also the most dangerous, with daily demands that stretch me to the limits of my strength and courage. From the first day in our kayaks to the last week, just before reaching the Mediterranean, there are a series of potentially fatal mishaps. The following stories describe the closest calls of this incredible journey and some of the invaluable life lessons taken from these experiences.

Although Lake Victoria, in Uganda, is generally recognized as the main source of the Nile, I was always intrigued by the fact that the Kagera River in Burundi is its most important tributary, supplying more water to the lake than any other source except direct rainfall. When we arrive in Uganda, officials tell us no one has ever traveled down the Kagera to the lake and that it passes largely through uninhabited wilderness. This was wonderfully appealing information from the standpoint of pure exploration. I suggest to Jean and André that we add a great adventure to our expedition by beginning near the headwaters of the Kagera in Burundi, a small country bordered by Tanzania, Congo and Rwanda, and then down the river to Lake Victoria and continue from there. My companions are in complete agreement and become as eager as I am to start.

When we arrive in Burundi, we meet with the local

district commissioner, a slender, gray-haired gentleman whose headquarters are only sixty miles from the Kagera. When I describe to him our plan to descend the river, he feels compelled to warn us of the dangers we will face.

"I wish you chaps would reconsider this idea of boating down the Kagera," he says. "I've lived twelve years hereabouts, and no one I know, African or not, can tell you much of anything about the country, let alone the river. There are swarms of hippos everywhere though—bloody awful beasts when they're stirred up. If they tip you in the drink, they'll either finish you off higgledy-piggledy, or the crocs will snatch you up before you can crawl out. The rapids are devilish, too, and—"

And I think, *Here we go again.* But I listen patiently as he finishes cataloging the disasters awaiting us. Finally he asks to see our boats, and when he sees our disassembled kayaks lying in the bottom of the truck, he is appalled. "You can't mean you're going to try for Lake Victoria in these toys!"

André speaks only a little English and Jean none at all, so it is my duty to answer. He is even more dismayed when I say, "Not only to Lake Victoria, but right on down the Nile to Egypt." And then we explain our expedition.

"I can't give you my official permission," he finally answers gravely. "If you and your partners insist on doing the Kagera, you do so entirely on your own responsibility. All I can say is I hope you make it." And then we return to pleasant conversation for a few moments. He drives off with a warm farewell, "Cheerio and good luck! Don't forget to send me a full report. I'll be anxious to know how you make out."

The first morning on the banks of the Kagera dawns hot and clear. We are so anxious to get under way that we dispense with breakfast. We assemble our boats, carefully fitting and locking the various sections together and then inserting the frames into the canvas skins. We carry the slender shells down the steep bank and through a jungle of towering emerald-green papyrus to the river's edge. Several more trips suffice to fit our four hundred pounds of equipment into waterproof bags and load four bags aboard each kayak.

I give André my Luger pistol and Jean the .22 caliber rifle. I keep the 12-gauge shotgun so that each of us has a weapon for emergencies. Then, with everything securely lashed inside, André and Jean set their boats into the silty water, jump in and push off into the brown flood, while I film their departure from the bank. The Kagera, one of the swiftest rivers in Africa, sweeps them downstream and out of sight before I can pack my camera away.

Eager to catch up and excited to begin the river journey, I push off into the river—and then am startled almost out of my wits by the sudden, violent splashing of a huge bull hippo bobbing to the surface just ahead of me, blowing and snorting and forcing me to swerve close to the papyrus to dodge him. My naive opinion that an unprovoked hippo is not dangerous to man is refuted when this great barrel-shaped hulk plunges after me in a vicious charge that leaves no doubt as to his intentions. He is nearly as long as my kayak and must weigh three tons, yet his rage at my invasion of his territory drives him through the water at an incredible speed. His nostrils blast spray with every snort, and his huge yellow tusks are, to say the least, horrific!

Fear sets my arms flailing like a windmill in a gale, the double blades of my paddle churning the water to froth. I pull ahead slowly until, at last, the angry hippo breaks off his pursuit and drops back, content that he has evicted the intruder from his domain. I tremble with adrenaline and relief—but then notice that about a hundred yards ahead, a whole family of hippos are strung across the river in a formidable blockade. At the rate I am being swept along by the current, I can't avoid them, but I paddle toward the widest gap and hope I can get through before any of them close in on me. With a few quick, hard strokes I am able to streak through, leaving behind a group of very astonished "river horses."

At the head of a stretch of rapids I at last catch up with Jean and André, who are also unnerved by hippo encounters. André has counted 112 of the beasts.

And then we encounter the rapids, a short and tricky stretch that provides a chilling new experience for André and me—one that quickly teaches us how little we are prepared for white water. Though André and I have traveled in our kayaks on the Marne and Seine rivers in France, we haven't run any white water. Jean, on the other hand, is a skilled paddler from his years of kayaking on prominent rivers in France and Germany. Prudently, André and I let Jean lead so that we can imitate his techniques.

Wearing heavy dark glasses, with his nylon hat jammed on tightly and strapped securely around his chin, Jean appears supremely calm as he strokes along, correcting his course with expert little dips and pulls of his paddle. By contrast, André and I are ham-handedly awkward—too often overreacting in our nervous maneuverings. My kayak is so tippy I have the sensation of being on a tightrope. To keep from listing, I reposition the bags and sit squarely on the hard rubber seat. The heavy cargo makes the boats sluggish and hard to maneuver around the masses of rock confronting us, but at last we shoot through the rapids with only a few minor tears in the rubber hulls.

Just past the rapids, the hippos begin appearing again, and their unpredictable actions keep me in a state of hypertension. One monstrous old bull snorts and submerges as I glide toward him. A moment later I sweep by his position, hugging the solid wall of papyrus as close as I dare, every nerve in my body jangling. Just as I begin to relax, he rears to the surface only a few feet behind, lunging along in my wake in an obvious attempt to finish me off. I have read graphic accounts of hippo attacks in which boats have been smashed and paddlers mangled beyond recognition. My frail kayak seems ridiculously vulnerable, and again I race for my life, whipping the little craft over the water as fast as my aching arms can paddle.

For twelve miles we dodge hippos, discovering that while they're curiously amusing when viewed from the deck of a large launch or from the shore, they can be terrifying when one is in a fragile midget boat among them. At times it seems as if I am right in the water with them, positioned as I am with the seat of my kayak below the waterline and the top of the cockpit a scant eighteen inches above. There is a momentary break in the tension when I pass a trio of hippos lolling in the shade of the papyrus. They raise their heads in amazement as I sweep by, and I stare back in equal fascination, for one of them is a rare freak, an albino—not white, of course, but a light, glowing pink. The exhilaration I feel at being whisked along on the sweeping current changes to alarm as it occurs to me what a precarious position we are in: the three of us racing single-file down a slender, hippo-infested corridor framed by impenetrable twelve-foot walls of verdant papyrus, with no place to land and no way of stopping without capsizing. It is like a ski jump— no stopping until the end. And for us, the end comes as a stark catastrophe.

Soon, the wind blowing toward us carries the lusty sound of a big cataract ahead. I can't see it, however. Instead, all that is visible is a dark green barricade of lush vegetation that seems to block the entire river. Yet the current seems to sweep straight into the cul-de-sac. As I come closer, I see that the obstruction consists of two little islands, with interlacing vines and branches bridging the gap between them.

Can I possibly plow through the ivy-choked channel between the islands, or should I try to squeeze between the right bank and the first island? A pile-up is inevitable if all three of us hold to the same course. So I gesture with my hand and shout back at them, "Take the right channel," trying to sound more confident than I felt. And as I head straight into the jungle, I lay back as far as I can to avoid the tangle of vines and limbs clogging the narrow passageway.

The most hellish moments of my life up to this point then begin. Just as I flatten myself on the bottom of the kayak, it suddenly crashes to a halt deep within the growth. Submerged roots snag my boat, causing it to heel over sharply. Instantly, the torrent rushes over the tilted craft, filling and engulfing it. As the kayak settles, it turns turtle and breaks free of the vines.

I find myself being dragged along upside-down in the seething water. I try to break free, but my legs are ensnared in the lashings that secure the gear. Though I have been a free diver from the age of twelve, and have good lung capacity, I am in poor condition for the heart-bursting ordeal that follows. For several days, I have been suffering from an attack of dysentery that has sapped my vitality, and what strength remains has been squandered in the exhausting escapes from the charging hippos. Worse, the shotgun, which has been wedged between bags of equipment in the bow, breaks free and strikes me in the face, leaving me dazed and bloodied.

When my senses clear, I force myself to make one last attempt to break free and, using all my strength, finally manage to escape. As I kick away from the kayak I am seized by the madly swirling river, which bowls me along with such overwhelming force that I am completely powerless and too disoriented to determine the direction of the surface. I am sweeping along like a piece of driftwood, rolling from one turbulence to another, scraping over reefs, colliding with rocks—desperately fighting to get my head above water.

The raging current tears at my hat, and the strap, still tightly fastened around my chin, is strangling me. With both hands I tear the hat off, fleetingly regretful as I think of myself bareheaded under a burning African sun. Then it occurs to me that sunstroke is the least of my worries at the moment. My heavy boots are dragging me down like lead weights. I claw at them frantically to tear them from my feet, but I can't do it. I am drowning. *So this is the way I go,* I thought, *like a fly sucked down a drain.*

Then, as I silently cry out, *Dear God, please help me!* my head breaks the surface just as my lungs are ready to explode. For a glorious moment, I breathe in delicious gulps of air before I am sucked under again; but the brief respite is all that I need. I feel a sudden flush of rage at being imprisoned in the grip of the violent current, and with an overwhelming urge to survive, I fight back to the surface again. Using only my arms, since kicking with my feet only seems to make matters worse, I manage to keep from going under again.

As I sweep along downstream the river becomes less turbulent, though the current is still brutally strong. I begin to wonder how long it will be before the crocodiles come after me. Just then I catch a momentary glimpse of the river behind me and see the dangerous stretch of rapids I have just survived. Jean and André are nowhere to be seen.

I work my way toward the right bank, and after several attempts, I am finally able to grip stalks of papyrus and haul myself out of the racing torrent. I collapse on a floating mass of decaying vegetation, gasping for air and feeling half-dead from fatigue.

Through waves of nausea, I feel a jolt, then hear an anxious French voice asking if I am all right. It is Jean. I roll toward him and gasp, "I think so. Where's André?" His only answer is to hold up a sodden hat and one dripping bag. André had capsized, and we can only assume he has drowned. We have lost one of our company and two-thirds of our irreplaceable equipment. The ambitious French-American Nile expedition appears to be ended at its very beginning—and after only one month in Africa. "Send me a report," the district commissioner had said, but the report we'll have to send him now will only confirm his dire warnings.

When I have enough energy, I flounder through the jungle of papyrus and undergrowth to the high rocky bank, crawl on hands and knees to the top, and begin searching for our lost comrade, while Jean crosses the river to do the same on the opposite bank. I shuck off my water-soaked boots and shirt to make the going easier and then pick up a game trail along the bank and follow it upstream toward the roar of the rapids. Stumbling and nearly falling many times, I fight to throw off the effects of my ordeal. Half paralyzed from exhaustion, I scarcely have control over my body. My ears, clogged with water, ring and throb. I have trouble focusing my eyes. I have to stop and vomit up the stomachful of silty water that I swallowed, further closing the stricture in my throat that causes me to gasp for air. I stagger along back to the two islands, where the ordeal began, without finding any sign of André.

Then, exhausted as I am, I feel a brief sense of elation as I spy my kayak at the foot of the cascade, bottom up against a reedy bar. It seems largely intact; we may be able to go on after all.

Ignoring the boat for the moment, I join Jean in shouting for André. We call and search for more than an hour. André has vanished. The only sounds are from the clamorous rapids and the monkeys chittering in the trees. Nothing can be seen but the boiling flood sweeping through the papyrus below us and hundreds of black swallows milling over the surface of the river, making little splashes as they skim and dart. The evidence points to a dreadful certainty that I can't bring myself to accept—that André has drowned and his body is being swept away downstream.

We postpone the search temporarily to salvage my kayak before it can break away from its resting place. I am on the right bank; the boat is on the left. To reach it I have to swim the river, a prospect that, not surprisingly, fills me with terror. But, steeling myself, I slip into the river upstream of the boat and use the current to help me across, alert for a crocodile attack.

Jean and I splash to the islet, right the boat and drain out the water. I open the "waterproof" camera case and find it half-filled with water, and my camera—the sixteen-millimeter Ciné Special with five lenses—soaked. And five hundred feet of color film containing irreplaceable footage lays ruined and exposed under inches of murky water. Now my first filming effort is spoiled, and the movie camera, one of the finest available, is out of commission. The nearest place that we can have the camera and lenses cleaned and renovated is Nairobi, Kenya—more than seven hundred miles away.

After our salvage operation, I force myself to climb into my kayak and push off, heading downstream to where Jean has beached his boat at a hippo wallow. But I still don't trust the treacherous river. By snatching hold of the solidly rooted papyrus every few yards, I am able to control my speed and prevent the current from capturing the kayak. I have a scare when my nervous grabbings nearly cause my delicately balanced craft to tip over. At last, with pounding heart, I nose into the gloomy runway in the tall green sedge.

How can I face André's family and tell them what has happened?

At that moment, I hear Jean crashing through the thick brush above the reeds. He bounds up to me with a whoop of joy, announcing that he has found André! He rushes to his kayak and we ferry across the river, then leave our boats and hurry up the very trail that I took in my fruitless search for André. After reaching the rapids, we plow our way through a bog to the water's edge, where I look out over the thunderous cascade and see a stranded André nonchalantly waving to us from a mass of rock a hundred feet from shore, where he has crashed his kayak. We haven't seen André before because he has smashed into a rocky islet in the center of a blind spot, where the right bank forms a horseshoe curve around the rapids. He hasn't heard our shouts over the roaring water, and as he tells us later, he is afraid we have perished when we don't show up. At last, he saw Jean searching for him—but Jean hadn't heard his shouts, either, and André attracted his attention only by tying his blue bandanna to a long stem of papyrus and waving it in the air.

It is a tremendous relief. I'd been blaming myself for the whole disaster, because it had been my idea to start our journey from the headwaters of the Kagera rather than at the Victoria Nile. But the disaster hasn't been so terrible after all—no loss of life.

Now we have to get André off of the reef in the middle of the rapids. We have him tie a rock to the end of his kayak mooring line and throw it to us; we then anchor the line firmly around a clump of papyrus. André settles down in his badly damaged boat and gingerly pushes away from the rocks, and we begin reeling him in like a hooked tuna as the racing torrent tears at the frail craft.

We have pulled him almost to shore when his kayak, its back broken in the collision with the rocks, folds at the center, allowing the rushing water to flood in and engulf it. André spills out but makes a lucky grab for the rope just in time to keep from being carried away. While Jean plunges through the dense papyrus to help André out of the water, I hold fast to the line, my arms nearly pulled out of their sockets by the swamped boat. When I can't hold on a moment longer, André heaves himself out of the water and begins helping Jean with the kayak.

We try to rest then, lying on a mattress of cushy reeds, but a hotbed of hungry insects soon stings us into activity. We stamp a path through the forest of obstinate papyrus, then wrestle the battered boat and the waterlogged baggage up the rocky wall of the gorge to the dry land above. We are exhausted by the exertion of wallowing and staggering with our loads in knee-deep muck, but the real misery comes when squadrons of kamikaze insects attack our exposed flesh. It seems that every creeping, flying vampire in the area has come to prospect our bodies for a meal, stilettoing us from ears to ankles until we are a mass of stinging, itching welts. It is the longest and most painful day of our lives.

We build a big fire with heavy branches, lay out all the damp equipment on the coarse grass around it, then collapse in a stupor onto our sleeping bags. We are covered with chigger, tsetse fly and mosquito bites and smarting from scratches caused by thorns and sawgrass. André and I have numerous painful bruises from our capsizings in the rock-bound rapids, but the single most overpowering emotion we feel is tremendous gratitude to still be alive.

From the moment I awake on the morning after our accident, I luxuriate in the delicious feeling of just being alive. I always feel great relief in surviving a "close call," but never have I been left with such a deep sense of *joie de vivre* as that possessing me as a result of my intimate flirtation with death on the Kagera. Never before has the fundamental fact of existence—to be alive and in full possession of my faculties—seemed such a profound blessing. The discouragement I feel at our setback evaporates under the flush of this new inspiration. I resolve to nourish it through the remaining years of my life and, like so many of the Africans I have come to love and respect, live each day to the fullest, with optimism and keen awareness, as if it were my last! The famous poem "Look to This Day," from ancient India, captures the essence of these feelings:

> *Look to this day, for it is Life, the very Life of Life;*
> *In its brief course lie all the verities and realities of our existence,*

The bliss of growth,
The glory of action,
The splendor of beauty,
For yesterday is already a dream, and tomorrow is but a
*   vision;*
But today well-lived makes every yesterday a dream of
*   happiness,*
And every tomorrow a vision of hope.
Look well, therefore, to this day.
Such is the Salutation of the Dawn.

We remain encamped by the Kagera for four days, drying out, getting our gear back in order and exploring the great game-filled wilderness surrounding us.

Unlikely as it seems, we come to regard our Kagera disaster as a lifesaving event—a miraculous, though painful, reprieve from certain death. This outlook emerges one day as André and I are hiking through the bush along the river, intent on making a reconnaissance of the unknown land around the upper Kagera. We come upon a sight that chills us—a murderous, absolutely impassable rapid, where the river churns through a narrow defile in an avalanche of angry water that sucks and leaps around several big boulders strewn over its course. Here nature has created a treacherous booby trap, camouflaging the wild, rock-choked rapids with snarls of lianas and creepers that drape down from tall trees and dance on the brown flood. So perfect is the concealment that a man approaching this deadly ambush in a kayak would not recognize it in time.

If not for our accident, which has so abruptly terminated

our Kagera trip, we would have been swept on unsus-pectingly and smashed against the boulders, sucked under and finished off. Ironically, the only way our lives could have been spared was for us to have been stopped, abruptly and decisively, where we were shut down—at the little islands upstream. Thus, our disaster, though extremely dangerous, has been a godsend in disguise.

Late one afternoon, as I am tramping through the tall grass near our tent, I suddenly come face-to-face with a grazing hippo. He gives me a surprised grunt, wheels around and heads for the river at a fast jog. Every year hippos kill many people in Africa, a large percentage of them on land, so it seems a wise idea to keep my speci-men on the run before he gets any pugnacious ideas and reverses his course. I let out a blood-curdling whoop and charge after him at top speed. I already know that hippos are marvelously fast swimmers, but it seems incredible that on land, with no water to support their ponderous bulk, they can also be swift runners. Yet pounding after him all the way back to the river, I can't keep up with him—much less close the gap between us.

I don't give up the chase until the hippo, his stumpy legs driving like pistons, plunges headlong into the river and disappears under the waves. It is a foolhardy stunt, but with a certain poetic justice to it. And how refreshing it is to be the pursuer for a change, rather than the pursued!

The next day, while rambling through the countryside, again alone, I come upon a hippo runway about one hun-dred feet long—a passageway forged through dense papyrus and reeds, leading straight to the river. Thirstier than usual, I follow the shadowy tunnel to the water's edge for a drink. The vegetation arches overhead above the runway, providing relief from the fierce sun. Though the air is heavy with pungent hippo musk I drink deeply, scooping up the flat-tasting water in double handfuls until I am satisfied.

Suddenly I hear a frightening sound as I turn to go back—a hippo is entering the tunnel and tramping rapidly toward me. Perhaps my scent has alarmed him as he grazed nearby, sending him dashing for the security of his more natural environment, the river. I feel trapped, fenced in by the solid walls of growth on either side, with the swift river at my back and a charging hippo bearing down on me like a giant bowling ball racing toward a single pin.

Just in time I spot a gap in the dense vegetation near me and dive through to safety as the excited animal sweeps past and crashes into the water with a mighty splash.

LIFE GOAL #1: *Explore the Nile River*

The Adventure of a Lifetime

Though temporarily discouraged by our near-fatal mishap on the Kagera River, Jean, André and I are as determined as ever to make the Nile expedition a success. From the beginning, we knew there would be serious difficulties during the long and hazardous journey, but we were in agreement that we would overcome each one and never abandon our goal of exploring the Nile all the way to the Mediterranean.

After getting reorganized and having the water-soaked camera repaired, we travel to the Nile's major source, vast Lake Victoria. The dimensions of this inland sea are astounding—two hundred miles long and 170 miles wide.

It is the world's second largest freshwater lake, with an area of 26,700 square miles, half again as big as Switzerland!

As an adventurous teenager, I had made a list of 127 goals that I committed myself to achieve during my lifetime. Goal number sixty-eight was "to swim in Lake Victoria." I fulfilled this ambition by taking a refreshing dip in the cool, milky-green water of the lake in one of its calm bays.

After two days of exploring the grassy shores, on foot and by Land Rover, we proceed to the northernmost point of Victoria. It is here that the Nile is created in the lake's only overflow. We hike along the hilly western banks to enjoy a superb panorama and our first view of the Nile. At times, during the months ahead, the river would devastate us with some of the most tortuous experiences we had ever known and yet, at other times, provide us with many of the most fulfilling and extraordinary events of our lives. We are awed into silence by the spectacle of the Nile below us, sweeping majestically out of the lake as a broad, fully formed river, to begin its interminable march through Uganda, Sudan and Egypt, and finally to flow into the blue Mediterranean. My thoughts turn to the first white man to discover this marvel, the English explorer (and one of my teenage heroes), John Hanning Speke, who came here on July 28, 1862, and solved one of the most ancient and perplexing mysteries of geography—the main source of the Nile. At last, I knew what he must have felt!

We investigate the river several miles downstream, struggling through rank jungle growth that becomes increasingly impassable. Along the way, we encounter several stretches of violent rapids. The barrier forces us to move on to the little steamer port of Namasagali, on the east bank of the Nile, a few miles downstream from the last of the unnavigable white water.*

Before leaving for Namasagali, we wired our kayak manufacturer in Paris to order new sections of framework to repair André's broken kayak, and gave instructions to ship them to Juba, a small town on the Nile in southern Sudan. We plan on covering the five hundred miles to Juba using our two intact boats and a small African dugout to replace the damaged kayak.

In Namasagali we meet Korfu, an educated young African of the Basoga tribe who speaks fluent English. He obligingly escorts us around nearby Basoga fishing camps, to act as interpreter and to help us purchase the dugout.

The Basoga are a proud tribe of water-lovers, some of the most skilled boatmen in Africa. On the riverbank, we watch several husky tribesmen, wearing only loincloths, busily at work putting finishing touches on a long, sleek, racing *piroque,* skillfully carved from a single jungle tree and painted with festive green and red designs. Other

---

*Just a year later, Jean Laporte returned to the Nile to produce a motion picture documentary and to kayak this stretch below Lake Victoria. Also, he wanted to film the 125 miles of river between Nimule and Juba, which he had been forced to miss because of illness. He was accompanied by a French ethnologist, Jacques Blein. The two launched their kayaks at the head of the deadly stretch of white water below Lake Victoria. Less than ten miles downstream, both men capsized as they attempted to paddle over a low waterfall, and Blein was swept away and lost. Later, Jean was informed by villagers that he was undoubtedly snatched up by the man-eating crocodiles that infested the river in that area.

men sit on the ground mending twine fishnets. Scarcely pausing in their work, the fishermen politely but firmly turn down our most generous offers to buy one of their dugouts. We receive the same response from all the other river men we speak with.

We hadn't anticipated any trouble in locating a dugout to replace André's kayak, but after three days we are still unsuccessful. We soon discover that, next to his wife, a Basoga considers his boat his most valuable and prized asset. It requires weeks of chipping, controlled burning and chiseling to produce one, and no amount of money is as important to a Basoga fisherman as his dugout.

We begin to mull over the last-ditch alternative of doubling up in one of the kayaks when the port captain solves the problem by introducing us to two smiling Jaluo Africans. The men are so adventurous that, even though they have never paddled down the river more than twenty miles from their village, they are willing to make a river safari with us in their big *mutumbi* or dugout, all the way to Masindi Port, 106 miles downstream. From there they can return home by means of the small steamer that plies between Namasagali and Masindi. The owner of the dugout, a tall, gravel-voiced man with the Neanderthal name of Oumu, acts as spokesman, while his short, mild-mannered partner, Gabrini, stands solemnly silent by his side as we work out details. Finally, our plan is set!

The next morning we have an audience of two dozen fascinated Basoga, who watch as we assemble our two useable kayaks and set them in the river. Eruptions of lightning blaze across a leaden sky, producing loud thunderclaps as we transport André's battered kayak and the rest of the baggage into the dugout, then push off. Our small flotilla makes a colorful sight as we move downstream. The two little satellite kayaks, bearing Jean and André, nimbly lead the way for the ponderous mutumbi, with Oumu steering in the stern, and Gabrini and me paddling vigorously in the waist.

Dugout on Lake Kyoga, with Oumu, André Davy and Gabrini.

Oumu's rough-hewn dugout is a reflection of his care-free personality. It is a disreputable-looking wreck of a boat that appears as though it has been hacked out of a deformed tree trunk by an apprentice carver with deli-rium tremors. A long, crooked branch jammed into a hole in the prow serves as a mast, with two mismatched sec-tions of ragged cloth tied on as a sail. Working side by side, "Gabby" and I chant little duets to keep time with our strokes. Neither he nor Oumu can speak English, but he picks up melodies quickly. Gabby's favorite is the "Song of the Volga Boatman," and he is lustily "yo-ho-hee-hoeing" in his quavering tenor as I sing in my deepest bass voice. Oumu never joins in our songfests, but sits in the stern as helmsman, grinning in appreciation.

Toward dusk the stillness of the river's silence is broken by the sounds of male voices. Behind us, tearing down-stream at top speed, is the trim racing dugout we had watched being constructed at Namasagali, the seven-man crew stroking their paddles in time to the rhythmic chant of the stern paddlers. It is a thirty-five foot beauty, with a pair of impala horns now affixed to the curving prow. In past years, when the tribes still warred with each other, it would have been a war canoe headed for battle. It races past us as if we were anchored in place, the sleek pirogue lunging forward with each powerful stroke of the coordinated paddles, and it soon disappears into the dis-tant haze.

Thirty-five miles downstream from Namasagali, we enter Lake Kyoga, an amoeba-shaped body of water. The Nile flows sluggishly through this shallow lake for sixty miles, losing millions of gallons of water in the spongy marshes bordering its shores.

As I paddle the dugout with Oumu and Gabrini, I no longer feel like a man of the modern world. I am a kindred spirit to Stone Age man, borne along in one of the most elemental and ancient forms of transportation ever conceived. A muscle-powered, carved-out tree trunk, directly descended from the oldest boat yet discovered—an eight-thousand-year-old dugout exhumed from a bog in Holland.

We stroke along without conversation for hours, surrounded by a trackless lotus-land of marshes with a sweeping immensity of blue sky overhead. The only sounds to break the eerie stillness are the soft rhythmic splashes of our paddles dipping into the green water, the whisper of a soft breeze and the occasional haunting cry of an ibis.

The first night of Kyoga we are unable to locate any dry land for a campsite, so we are forced to sleep in our cramped boats. We awake stiff and sore, peppered with mosquito bites. Jean takes a turn in the Mutumbi, while André and I set off in the kayaks.

Most of the day, I paddle alone, well ahead of the others, to observe the varied life of the lake.

I enjoy every sight along the way: a flight of vultures gracefully riding a thermal high overhead; the flash of red and iridescent green as a sunbird darts past; the wind dancing over the lake's surface, creating a kaleidoscope of patterns; and the whirr of blue dragonflies hovering around me. Kingfishers are frequent companions and create a vivid sight with their dark blue wings, cinnamon-colored bodies and red legs. They hover like toy helicopters, fifteen feet above the water, then arrow down in a splash of color and spray, to seize a small fish swimming too close to the surface.

In the late afternoon, I wait for my friends to catch up with me, and we continue together, searching the northern lakeshore in vain until nightfall for some kind of passage through the lush papyrus. Then we hear the nerve-wracking, tuba-like bellowing of several hippo, resounding out over the lake from the distance ahead.

Unable to find a landing, we are forced to move on into the sinister darkness of the starry, but moonless, hippo-haunted night—tightening our formation in hopes of achieving greater safety in numbers. Before traveling to Africa I had regarded the hippo as the most laughable clown in the animal world—everything about it comical, a cartoonist's delight. This impression is quickly reversed as a result of our personal experiences and the repeated warnings from wildlife experts who are unanimous in telling me that hippos kill more people in Africa than does any other animal—more than two hundred annually.

I'm well aware that a hippo's enormous scoop-shovel of a mouth, with its sharp upper and lower canines, can easily, with one crunch, fracture the back of a lion or a crocodile—or even a fragile kayak or dugout!

A bolt of fear shoots through me as a ghostly shape materializes out of the gloom—a lone hippo coming at us through the dimly lit water, shattering the still night with raucous bellows. We lay to with our paddles as fast as we can, but the heavy mutumbi moves at a maddeningly slow pace. André and I have to force ourselves to slow down and stay with our companions, hoping that a larger group might confuse or even intimidate the hippo. We are relieved to discover that he is more curious than aggressive, for he tags along behind us at a respectable distance, then vanishes into the darkness as abruptly as he had appeared. I am baffled at the number of hippos still swimming around in the lake in the dark. Normally hippos emerge from the water at night to feed on land. They forage overland, sometimes for miles, to graze on sweet grasses and succulent plants, consuming two or three hundred pounds of vegetation before returning to the water for their daytime aquatic life.

During the day, we had been able to spot herds of hippos in the distance and detour around them, but in the night, illuminated only by starlight, we grope ahead blindly, feeling uncomfortably vulnerable. I turn in different directions, in a state of suspense, but fail to get an accurate fix on the location of the numerous hippos in the lake and along the shores. We can hear them splashing around us, frighteningly close, sometimes blowing noisily as they surface after a dive.

Their grunts and snufflings reverberate through the dark as though amplified in an echo chamber. Some are inconsiderately silent, and André, a few yards away, suddenly shouts in fright as a hippo bumps into his kayak, splashing water all over him.

I sit rigidly erect, clutching the long aluminum paddle

with a viselike grip, my muscles twitching with fatigue from the long hours of nonstop paddling.

My body aches all over from the unbearable tension caused by the threat of a hippo charge. I am skimming over the black surface of a mysterious lake, in the flimsiest of boats, a cockleshell kayak, with no landmarks or even the light of a friendly campfire to guide us. I have a heavy foreboding of doom—a feeling that this could be the last night of our lives. It feels like passing through a minefield, with any one of a dozen or more hippo capable of destroying us in one violent attack.

Two hours after André's encounter, a quartet of hippos loom up to challenge us, snorting indignantly at our intrusion into their domain. Moving in close, they first threaten Jean and the two Africans, helpless in the unmaneuverable dugout. André and I return and divert the hippos' attention, successfully drawing them off, but having to paddle as fast as we can to keep beyond them. Three quickly give up the chase, but the fourth hippo pursues us closely for several minutes, viciously intent on our destruction. Our paddles churn the water to froth as we put on the necessary burst of speed to escape, and still we only barely manage to elude him.

At last, exhausted, we tie our boats to some papyrus stalks at a small island, fit ourselves among the baggage, and quickly fall asleep. It is midnight, and we have been paddling nonstop for nearly fifteen hours.

By early afternoon the next day we arrive at Masindi Port, where a small wood-burning paddlewheeler is tied up at the dock. The captain, a solidly built white man about forty years old, barefoot and clad only in khaki shorts, waves to us from the upper deck. As we land, at least sixty villagers stand along the bank to watch our arrival and to greet us with hearty "Jambos."

My legs nearly buckle as I jump ashore. Twenty-seven hours of being confined in my kayak, without a single step on shore, has left them stiff and rubbery, and I have little control over them. My paddling muscles throb, and I am painfully sunburned since my uniform of the day has been only khaki shorts. I am a few pounds lighter—but altogether I am in fine shape and eager for the next adventure.

We have timed our arrival perfectly—the captain had been ready to leave, and we are able to persuade him to wait a half hour longer so that Oumu and Gabrini would have time to arrive, ship their dugout on board the steamer and ride back home, instead of having to paddle all the way back upriver to Namasagali. The captain invites us to his cabin, where he pours a brandy for André and himself and a lemon squash for me to toast our safe arrival. "How are you making out with the hippos, chaps?" he asks. When we describe our adventures with them on the Kagera River and on Lake Kyoga, he shakes his head and says: "You don't know how lucky you've been up to now."

He relates a harrowing hippo story—an experience he'd had the year before while traveling in a small motor launch near the mouth of the Kagera. He and a caucasian friend and three African crewmen were cruising along when an angry hippo attacked them. Before they could maneuver out of range, the hippo began chomping away at the stern of the boat with his great yellow tusks.

Unsatisfied, he submerged under the launch, then lurched upward toward the surface so violently that the craft keeled over and capsized, spilling everyone into the water. There was a frenzied scramble to climb on top of the over-turned craft, all of them reaching it safely except one crew-man. He became trapped underwater and drowned.

Oumu, Gabrini and Jean land a few minutes later, and our African traveling companions break into smiles of happiness when we tell them the good news about their trip back. We hurriedly load them and their heavy mutumbi aboard, give them their well-earned bonus, shake their hands in farewell and then wave them off as the little paddle wheeler departs and churns upriver. There is a tinge of sadness to our abrupt and hurried part-ing—we have become genuinely fond of them during our days together, and it is with sincere regret that we watch them go, realizing that we will never see them again. But then, for me, sadness on parting from African friends, black and white, has been a frequent emotion, and always a painful experience throughout our journey. I meet and establish warm ties with special individuals whose friendship I would like to enjoy for a lifetime—then have to leave them forever only a short time afterwards. I have never learned to accept this gracefully or without a wrenching sense of loss.

LIFE GOALS #156 & #87: *Visit Lake Albert and Film Wild Elephant*

Five Tons of Fury

A few days later we arrive at Lake Albert, where the Nile is powerfully reinforced by the lake's northern overflow. We are able to arrange transportation for André and his equipment aboard the lake's paddlewheeler. The quaint little steamer was just headed for its home port of Pakwach, a short distance downriver, when we flagged it down and received permission from the captain for André to travel with him. Jean and I will camp on shore tonight, and continue tomorrow in our kayaks for a rendezvous with André at Pakwach.

We push off this morning under a leaden overcast against a gusty headwind but make steady progress as Lake Albert narrows into the Nile. On the left bank we spot some Africans and greet them, but on the right bank we see no sign of human life. Extending eastward from the Nile and covering many hundreds of square miles into the Sudan is a vast, virtually uninhabited region, abandoned by all but a few villages because of the scourge of the tsetse fly. The shoreline is grassy and low, with only an occasional hill covered by forests that have parched to yellow in the dry season.

A few miles before reaching Pakwach I sight four dark specks against the green and yellow shoreline far in the distance. They move as I watch them, and the binoculars confirm it: elephants! I turn to alert Jean, but he is far behind, so I move as close as I dare in my kayak, then pull into the papyrus. A crocodile slides into the water not far away as I

Children of the Alur tribe prepare to launch my kayak into Lake Albert for a trial ride.

creep out of the boat and sit crosslegged in the reeds beside my kayak, watching the huge elephants peacefully feeding, their spinal columns massive and prominent. I know that once they become aware of my presence they will probably move off. Fortunately, their vision is poor, and while their senses of hearing and smell are more acute than a dog's, I remain downwind, trying to be very quiet.

My patience is rewarded when they begin to drift toward me. They have sprayed themselves with water, which makes them darker than the elephant I had seen in the Tsavo Forest. Their trunks snake down to scoop up grasses, and though three of the elephants amble away, one of them wanders toward me—so close I can hear his stomach rumble as he feeds. With baggy knees and extensive wrinkles, his immense body appears enclosed in a loose gray robe that he has slept in. His trunk is marvelous in action: a fusion of nose and upper lip, weighing upward of three hundred pounds and moved by forty thousand tiny, separate muscles to make the trunk serve as a combination hand, arm, nose, suction pump, trumpet, snorkel and battering ram, able to tweeze a berry or toss around a half-ton log. The bull elephant coming toward me has three tick birds and two large white cattle egrets balanced blithely on his broad back, looking like five dignified commuters on their way to work.

The elephant turns, finally, and starts up the bank, giving me the chance I have been waiting for; I wind my Ciné, adjust the settings and then cautiously stalk my quarry, creeping forward at a half-crouch. I am afraid that at any moment the birds might give the alarm, but they remain silent. As I stand tensely watching, the elephant turns broadside, providing a more photogenic shot of his anatomy than the enormous hindquarters he has been presenting.

Then the elephant catches the sound of the camera whirring and faces me squarely. His trunk tests the air, swaying like an aroused cobra. He has not yet caught my scent. When I start to retreat, the great triangular ears shoot forward, then flap back along his head; he rocks nervously, shifting his weight from his left to his right legs

An angry elephant mounts the bank of the Albert Nile after charging me and chasing me into the river.

and back again in a funny little shuffling dance. Then he makes a short rush at me in what amounts to a sham charge, taking several quick, short steps forward and stopping suddenly, raising a small cloud of dust. There is nothing vicious in this action; it is like an old farmer shooing a trespassing chicken out of his garden. I can almost hear the elephant say, "Scat!"

He tries a sham charge twice again, giving me ample warning and time to escape. I keep eyeing my boat, figuring the fastest getaway—but still whirring away with the camera. Because I am holding my ground, the elephant's sense of privacy is completely outraged, and his charge this time is no sham. His ears fan out wide, winglike, his trunk goes down and curls back in the danger signal position, and he comes for me.

I rush to my kayak just as he charges. Cold fear now lending speed to my flight, I drop my camera in and wrench the boat into the river almost in one motion, scant seconds before the elephant comes thundering up. His momentum carries him knee-deep into the oozy shallows, where he stands shaking his great head and lashing the air with his trunk.

I am riding safely on the river a few yards from the tusker when Jean catches up. He picks up my camera and films a scene of me with my irritated friend, who has pulled himself out of the weed-choked water and is lumbering up the bank, turning our way every few feet to see what we are up to.

African elephants weigh up to six tons and stand as tall as eleven feet; yet despite their size they can move murderously fast. They have been clocked at twenty-five miles an hour. If I had been twenty-five feet farther from my kayak, I would never have reached it alive. As some consolation, however, if the elephant had trampled me to death, he would then probably have provided me with a decent burial under twigs and leaves. Included in the remarkable practices of elephant etiquette is the paradoxical custom of burying a freshly killed enemy. With his combination of cunning, speed and strength, many authorities consider the African elephant to be the world's most dangerous big game animal.

At Pakwach we have a wonderful stroke of luck when we meet and are befriended by the top chieftain of one of the prominent local tribes, the Banyoro. Chief Oubidu, a handsome, medium-sized man wearing a brown toga, arranges for two of his tribesmen and their dugout to travel with us 120 miles down the Albert Nile to the hamlet of Nimule. On the day of our departure, the chief supervises our purchases at his village open-air market: dried fish, beans, rice, bananas and a chicken, plus a supply of maize flour for the journey. Our boatmen, Okelo and Oliyo, are waiting for us at the river, in a small dugout whose bottom is already under two inches of murky water that seeps in from a crack in the starboard side of the stern. To my surprise, Okelo speaks some English and his brother understands Swahili. An entranced crowd from the village lines the high banks to see us off.

During our second night together, the Banyoros and I have several harrowing experiences with hippo. By dusk, we hadn't found a break in the dense wall of papyrus

lining the river, so we decide to push on to the nearest village, Obongi. André is in my kayak, Jean is in his, and I am
taking a turn in the pirogue. While Jean and André paddle
ahead to set up the tent and prepare supper, Oliyo and
Okelo and I dodge hippos in our sluggish mutumbi. What
had begun as a lovely tropical night now becomes oppres-
sive, as hippo after hippo challenges or charges us. Most of
the time we can hear only their grunts and splashings as
they come for us, but on two occasions lone hippo
approach close enough to be seen. The two Africans are
terrified by the monsters and join me in paddling furiously
to get out of their way. One hippo plunges toward us with
such violence that the waves created rock our boat dangerously. We have to quickly shift our weight to the high
side to keep from capsizing. Neither Okelo nor his brother
can swim. If the dugout had been upset, even if they had
survived the attack, they surely would have drowned.
When the hippos realize that we are not a threat, but are
moving rapidly away from them, they seem mollified and
back off. We finally sight Jean and André's campfire, a
cheery oasis in the darkness, and land, jubilantly relieved
that we have survived another trial by hippo.

The next day we come to a village of the Madi tribe—
the first settlement we have encountered on the east side
of the river since leaving Lake Albert. André and I have
been gliding along when we notice a prominent water-
way leading into the papyrus. We follow the rocky corridor past the jungle of sedge and come out into a tree-lined
pool below the village; a few huts nestle in a picturesque
setting of trees and granite hillocks. It is beautiful; the

men are friendly and talkative, though we understand nothing, and if the mosquitoes hadn't been so murderous, the campsite would have been ideal. As it is, we have to slaughter dozens in our tent before sleeping—and then the idyll is complete. Before we leave the village in the morning, I notice that interspersed among the huts are five granaries, large containers constructed of finely inter-woven dry grass and saplings, each with a cone-shaped lid, and containing one of the crops or food staples pro-duced by the people: cotton, peanuts, millet, manioc and *durra*. Okelo tells me that babies and young children are often hidden in the glorified baskets at night when there are leopards, hyenas or other dangerous animals on the prowl, or during an attack by enemy tribesmen.

Besides the human population, the village is also heavily populated with fat, gaudy orange and purple *agama* lizards that scuttle out of my way wherever I walk or sit, blinking at me with heads engagingly cocked, as if they were sizing me up.

The village turns out en masse this morning to see us off, everyone standing on a granite outcrop to watch as we float through the papyrus tunnel to the river. Our visit was probably the most unusual thing that had ever happened to them, and they want to savor it to the end.

I take another turn in the mutumbi. Okelo moans and says, "I happy with you, Bwana, but you make me work too hard and I get pains in heart." This from a man who has twice my stamina in rowing.

"My friend, you're just a twenty-four carat goldbrick," I tell him to his bewilderment. To distract him from his cardiac problems, I teach Okelo a little rhyme to paddle by. I composed this using the names of African places beginning with the letter K we have visited: Kitale, Kabale, Kisenyi, Kigali, Kitega, Kampala, Kagera. He soon had the syncopation down fine, but had trouble saying them in the right order.

As we near the Sudanese border the country becomes increasingly hilly and rocky, and for the first time we begin seeing date palms. We have another brush with hippos when we blunder into a dozing herd submerged next to a rocky island. We don't see them until they rear suddenly from the water. Okelo forgets the pains in his heart and nearly breaks his paddle in a mad effort to escape. But the hippos are sleepy and as surprised by us as we are by them. By pulling on our paddles with all our might we get away without incident. (I tried to keep count of the hippos I saw on the Albert Nile, but lost track at around 450.)

LIFE GOALS #157 & #158: *Experience an African Foot Safari and Visit Juba, Sudan*

Trekking Through an African Wilderness

Though prominently labeled on our maps, Nimule consists only of a corrugated iron customs shed and a few isolated huts beyond: a humble gateway to Sudan, Africa's largest nation. Along the 125-mile stretch between Nimule and Juba, the Nile is called *Bahr-el-Jabel,* Arabic for "River of the Mountain." It is a vigorous, rapids-filled torrent rushing downhill through a narrow valley, over a solid rock bottom almost all the way to Juba.

Since we know it would be disastrous to go down this violent expanse of the Nile in our thin-skinned kayaks, we decide that our best alternative is to trek on foot, following the river along the banks. The critical problem of transporting Jean, our kayaks and most of our equipment to Juba is miraculously solved when a white man appears on the road—a Mr. Jim Dodson, an English engineer working with the Sudan government. Jim is a real godsend. As we arrive at the remote outpost of Nimule, he comes rattling down the seldom traveled track in a cloud of dust, driving his light pick-up truck. In a lavish display of hospitality, he agrees to take Jean and our gear to Juba and then invites us to make his home our headquarters. Also, he helps immeasurably in getting our hike organized by driving us to the nearby village of Zelindo where he introduces us to his friend, the paramount chief of the Onandi tribe. The chief, an unusually tall man with the bearing of a general, agrees to assign three of his villagers to come with us as bearers on the long cross-country trek. Jean is too ill from an attack of bronchitis to accompany us. So while he recuperates at Jim's home, André and I, together with our spear-carrying bearers, Akim, Ogone and Sabi, set off down a game trail to begin an exciting eight-day, 125-mile foot safari through the wilderness of southern Sudan. I take the lead, carrying our only weapon besides the spears, a .22 rifle (our heavy firearms having been lost previously in the Kagera rapids), and a pack of equipment that includes our indispensable 16mm camera.

The five of us trek along in the traditional African safari style, single file, through the dense, ten-foot-tall elephant grass and thickly forested bush. I set a steady pace, picking out game trails that will keep us close to the river. We pass through a beautiful, unspoiled land, abounding with wildlife and populated by only a few small villages of

Shenzis—isolated villagers living a primitive hand-to-mouth, "survival of the fittest," kind of existence, virtually untouched by civilization. The slender winding game trails are our salvation in penetrating the dense jungles of otherwise impregnable tall grass and thorn bush. I sense an aura of menace whenever we enter one of these narrow corridors. There is just one entrance and one exit, with only a few feet of visibility ahead, and no escape on either side. I can't help but wonder what would happen if we should suddenly come upon something dangerous—a lion, or rhino or even a spitting cobra.

Our resolve to press on is seriously tested one morning as we round a bend in one of the winding passageways. I am in the lead, André next, followed by the three Africans. We come upon a large mound of Cape buffalo manure—so fresh it is still steaming in the hot sun. Our nerves are really on edge as we step around the pile, now covered with blue-green flies, and move down the path, hoping not to bump into the animal.

It is a scary situation: We are trapped by the double barrier of thick vegetation, with one of the most dangerous animals of Africa close by. Solitary bull buffalo have a notorious reputation for having a hair-trigger temper, one that explodes whenever they catch an individual on foot in their territory. When they do, they charge at top speed, twice that of a fleeing human, and smash into the victim with their massive horns, and inevitably fatal results. The bull never seems content with just killing a victim, but methodically butts, kneels down on and tramples the body with its fifteen-hundred-pound hulk until there is nothing left but a bloody mess. We are defenseless against a charging buffalo, as our only weapons are two spears and my little .22 rifle, with only a single bullet remaining.

I am surprised at the nervous reaction of the Africans. They have total confidence in my "pea-shooter" rifle, not having any concept of the weapon's caliber. To them, a gun, any kind of gun, is capable of killing anything it is aimed at. Yet they are immediately upset at the sight of the pile of dung, recognizing the threat it represents to our lives.

After about fifty yards of very suspenseful walking, we break out of the claustrophobic corridor into open country. I jump with fright as we emerge into the clearing— not from the appearance of the buffalo I have been half expecting to encounter, but by the panicky movements of a herd of beautiful, golden-brown impala. Startled by our sudden appearance, they bound across a shallow stream ahead of us in great splashy leaps and disappear into the bush. As we follow them across, I spot some well-defined hoof prints in the mud of the opposite bank where the buffalo has waded across before us. Newly alert, we tramp along for miles, through the rest of the day, without ever coming upon the beast.

That night, as André and I are sleeping in our tent near the river, Akim wakes us with disturbing news that a large animal is crashing around in the bush next to our camp. I get up to investigate and find Ogone and Sabi huddled around our fire, now built up into a roaring blaze. Their eyes are saucer-like with fright, and each one has his spear stuck in the ground at his side for instant use. Akim tells me they are sure it is the buffalo we had feared meeting in the bush that morning. But within a few minutes the mysterious prowler appears in the firelight, just thirty yards away. It is not the buffalo, but three thousand pounds of potential trouble: a full-grown black rhino!

We stand frozen at attention, breathlessly waiting for a possible charge.* Our nocturnal intruder shuffles around nervously for a few minutes, seemingly undecided what to do. For a moment, I wonder if he might carry out the old African folk tale that says that a night roving rhino will sometimes rush into a campsite and stomp out the campfire there with its big feet. But finally, probably intimidated by the leaping flames of our bonfire, he ambles off into the bush. We turn in again and sleep peacefully until we are abruptly awakened in the dead of night by the maniacal shrieking of a hyena, one of the most chilling sounds of the animal kingdom. It is even worse than the scream of a fire engine siren, particularly when it jolts you out of a deep sleep and is the first thing that impacts your consciousness. Generally hyenas avoid

---

*Of the "Big Five" animals of Africa, (which includes the elephant, Cape buffalo, lion and leopard), the black rhino is the most impetuous and least intelligent of them all. He possesses both an acute sense of hearing and smell, but is cursed with pathetically poor eyesight, unable to see clearly beyond a few yards. These characteristics, plus a volatile temperament, often result in his charging any unusual sound or movement near him, from a fluttering butterfly to a passing vehicle. His attacks are often sheer bluff, but a black rhino can be deadly when enraged, rocking along in a charge like an animated tank, at a speed of thirty-five miles an hour. Even when unprovoked, his behavior is unpredictable, particularly if he picks up a human scent in his territory. On the way to Lake Victoria, we came upon an overturned Austin car that had been rammed and tipped over by a black rhino, which had then gored the driver to death.

humans, but when goaded by hunger, they will frequently attack people sleeping outdoors.

And their attack is overpoweringly fatal. They have the strongest jaws of any carnivorous animal, able to crack an elephant's thighbone. When they pounce on a human victim they concentrate first on the face and neck, biting with such ferocity that in one ravenous chomp the face is removed and sometimes the entire head.*

I lay fully awake in my sleeping bag, aware of every rustle and crackling in the bush surrounding our tent. But the day dawns cloudless and hot, with no further sign of the hyena. That night we have an even more exciting experience when a herd of elephants surrounds our camp. We are awakened around midnight by the sounds of breaking tree limbs and stomach rumblings. The frightened Africans throw wood on the fire, and André and I quietly leave our tent to help them. We stand close to the fire, with our backs against a tree, listening intently as the herd feeds and waters just beyond us. The night is so dark our straining eyes can't make out a single elephant, but the noisy crashing, as the animals rip off branches or topple trees in order to feed off the leaves, conjures up a vivid picture of what is happening just beyond the flickering light cast by our campfire.

"If they come any closer," André whispers, "we're going to have to do some fast climbing."

---

*In certain regions of Africa, villagers dispose of their dead by leaving them in the bush for hyenas to feed on. But an occasional hyena, losing its fear of humans, will become a habitual man-eater, stalking and killing lone people.

"I doubt an elephant would have any trouble knocking this tree down," I answer. "Let's just hope there isn't a rogue in the herd that has a grudge against humans." Actually, it is thrilling being so close to the elephants, even though their nearness is a serious threat to our tent and equipment—and possibly even our lives. After a very long hour, during which time André and I offer up fervent petitions to the Almighty for protection, the herd gradually drifts away, enabling us to return to our beds.

The sixth day of our trek is the hottest day we have had since first landing in Africa. Shakespeare wrote, "All the world is cheered by the sun." But not when a person is hiking twenty miles a day under the full, unshaded blast of a Sudanese sun! The heavy air envelops us like superheated fog, causing us to pant like dogs. My heavy, broad-brimmed hat causes a steady flow of sweat to stream into my eyes and down my cheeks. Though burdensome, the hat is indispensable in protecting against heat stroke. Upon landing in Kenya the first advice I heard from local whites was: "Never go out during the heat of day without wearing a hat. Think of a cube of butter on your head!"

Sluggish from the heat, we march ahead at a slower pace than normal, André a few yards behind me and the barefooted Africans nimbly bringing up the rear. In spite of being unusually tired and fighting down a constant feeling of nausea, I am still happy to be traveling through one of the most extraordinary and isolated areas of Africa.

After months of living in the natural world, free from the bombardment of artificial stimuli, my senses are sharper than ever. I can see, hear and am aware of things that I would have been oblivious to in modern surroundings. I greatly enjoy observing the wildlife that our passing stirs up. Besides birds of every description, there are many vervet and blue monkeys in the trees and troops of olive baboons on the ground. A delicate little bush *duiker*, a species of antelope only two feet tall with a pair of tiny horns, shyly darts across the trail ahead of us and vanishes in the tawny grass.

During one of our rest stops, as I hunt for a passage to the river for a drink, I spot a long gray blotch on the sandspit of an island in midstream. It seems to be an outcropping of rock along the sand. When I move closer, I realize it is an enormous crocodile—at least three feet longer than my sixteen-foot kayak and twice as broad. Judging from his huge size, he must weigh more than a ton, the biggest crocodile I have seen since coming to Africa.

The great reptile lies there looking like a prehistoric creature. He shows no evidence of being alive. He doesn't move even when I climb down the riverbank, work my way through an opening in the papyrus to the water's edge and come within a stone's throw from him. I stare at him in awe, wondering about his age, which must be great, and whether he had eaten many humans. *How many African victims have contributed to your growth, old boy?* Knowing how fast crocs can move on land or in the water, I shudder at the thought of him coming after me, whether hiking along the riverbank or paddling my kayak on the Nile.

At dusk we camp between a pair of sheltering tamarind trees. André makes a fire and puts on a pot of rice and beans to cook for our dinner. Too weary to eat, I spread out my sleeping bag, crawl in and immediately fall into a deep sleep. A short time later I am shocked awake by a violent fit of uncontrollable shivering. It feels like I am being doused with a bucket of ice water. It is a warm night; why am I miserably cold? With chattering teeth, I open the equipment bag, which has been serving as my pillow, pull out all the extra clothing it contains and pack it around my trembling body. It doesn't help. The glacial chill comes from some deep, unreachable core inside me. I endure the discomfort of coldness much better than the mysterious transformation that comes over me about an hour later, when a hot flush sweeps over me. I quickly unzip my sleeping bag, cast off my cocoon of clothing and lay there naked, my body now burning with an intense fever that soon soaks the bag from the sweat pouring off of me. *What's happening to me?* Within a few minutes my body heat soars so high that I become concerned about the damage it might be doing to my brain. I try to sit up, thinking that I should go to the nearby river and lower my temperature by immersing myself in the cool water. But I don't have the strength. The most I can do is swig down large gulps of water from my canteen to keep from dehydrating, and then collapse back onto my bed to wait for the hot spell to pass. A wave of nausea causes me to throw up most of the water. The fever slowly subsides but is replaced by the worst headache I have ever known. The ground beneath me seems to spin until I am giddy. To turn my head or even move my eyeballs is intensely painful. There is no question now. I have a classic case of malaria. Of the various tropical diseases that we have been exposed to, this one worries me above all others because it is the one affliction that can force us to drastically change our plans.

Lying there on my sweat-soaked bag, my mind was oppressed by a sense of gloom. *What if I have the falciparum type of malaria?* This is the deadliest of the four forms of the parasitic disease—so lethal that it can kill a victim within hours after the first symptoms. *It would be bitterly ironic,* I thought, *if after all the ordeals we have survived since coming to Africa, that I might die as a result of some mosquito bites.* Even spared this horror, I know that any form of malaria weakens the entire body and drastically reduces energy levels. *How can I continue with the most physically demanding project of my life, one that continuously requires my full strength? How can I disappoint Jean and André if I'm unable to continue down the Nile with them, with more than three thousand miles still to travel?* These are some of the worrisome questions that disturb me just before I fall asleep.

Just after dawn, the men begin breaking camp, anxious to get moving again. I am in such bad shape that all I want to do is lie still and rest all day. Knowing this is not possible, I reluctantly get up, put on my khaki shorts, shoes and bush hat. There was no good reason to discuss details about my condition with André. We are running low on food and still have a long distance to cover over rough country before reaching Juba. "André," I say, "I've had a bad night. Why don't you and the men take the lead for a change and I'll follow along at my own pace?" With that, the Africans move off in front of André and me. Throughout the morning I stumble along in a daze, weak and uncoordinated, barely able to keep within sight of the others. I have the weird sensation that my head is detached from my body and just floating above it.

During the afternoon we detour around impregnable bush and tramp over a dry river bottom for a mile before returning to the Nile. The glare and heat radiating from the dazzling white sand gives me the blind staggers and come close to overpowering me. At one point I find myself on my hands and knees in the hot sand, feeling as though I have been bashed over the head with a club. I kneel there in a stupor, staring through the heat haze at my retreating companions as they thread their way, single file, through tall grass next to the river. Suddenly I feel totally alone and vulnerable. In crossing the riverbed I notice the tracks of a lion and those of several elephants. With no weapon to defend myself I know it is much safer to be with the group. The sharp sting of a tsetse fly biting my neck and drawing blood rouses me to action, the only time I actually welcome a bite from one of the little demons. I muster up enough strength to get to my feet and, though staggering like a drunk, manage to move ahead to catch up with my friends.

On the morning of the eighth and last day of our trek we come upon a broad footpath, the most well-defined trail we have seen since leaving Nimule. In the distance gray smoke billows from a rapidly expanding grass fire. We have no choice but to pass along the edge of the blaze. Akim leads us, skillfully picking his way over unburned areas. We hurry along, gasping and coughing from the acrid smoke, while flames crackle around us and fiery debris rains down, searing our skin and clothing. We soon emerge into clearer air and continue through a blackened landscape that steams and smolders in the brassy, smoke-filtered sunlight.

Reaching Juba

Late in the afternoon we reach the dusty outskirts of Juba. André and I look like emaciated jungle refugees. We are soot-stained from head to blistered toes, our eyes are bloodshot and ringed in dark circles, our lips are cracked, our beards scraggly, and our bare legs look like raw hamburger from the lacerating thorns and sawgrass. "Our own mothers wouldn't recognize us!" says André.

I pay off Akim, Ogone and Sabi, thanking them for their devoted services, then André and I head straight for Jim Dodson's home. We receive an enthusiastic welcome from our host and especially from Jean, who has been worrying about our safety on the long safari. André and I flip a coin to see who uses the metal bathtub first. I win and proceed to enjoy the most sensually satisfying bath of my life, despite the sting from abrasions all over my body.

André and I barely have the strength to dress after our baths. Jim generously arranges a special dinner to celebrate our successful trek, but we are too exhausted to eat much. Later in the evening I begin feeling terrible, as though my body has been able to postpone another major malaria attack until we have completed our foot safari and have reached our goal of Juba, where I could properly collapse. And collapse I do—right into bed. Jim quickly summons a Sudanese physician friend, Dr. Hassan Obbid, who administers medicine to treat my symptoms.

During the night I awake in a panic, desperately gasping for air, with a feeling of being slowly suffocated under a great weight. Jim, sleeping in the next room, is wakened by my strangled breathing and comes to sit beside the bed until the seizure eases off. I am so weak I can't turn over or lift my head from the straw pillow. A fear grips me that if I go to sleep again, I will stop breathing completely. Finally, unable to fight off sleep any longer and comforted by Jim's presence, I drift off into merciful slumber. For several days I am held captive in bed, too sick to get back into action. Every morning and evening Hassen, my solicitous doctor, stops by to dispense medicine and advice. (He also informs me that local government authorities are certain that André is the first Frenchman and I am the first American ever to make a foot safari over the 125-mile stretch between Nimule and Juba.) In the end he refuses, with great dignity, any compensation for all his professional services for the three of us and says, "It was a great honor to treat such unfearing explorers."

"Well, sorry to disillusion you, Hassen," I reply, "but I must confess that during the past three months I've experienced some of the most intense fear of my life!"

Double Jeopardy from Hippos and Crocs

Two weeks later we are underway on the Nile again. The combination of Dr. Obbid's effective medicines, plus ample food and rest, restore André to his usual energetic self. I have regained my strength, and Jean has recovered from his bronchitis. We repair André's damaged kayak with the new parts sent to us from Paris. It is wonderful paddling again, helped along by a steady four-knot current. The Nile here constantly fluctuates in width, at times narrowing to only about fifty yards, then, in other places, ballooning to more than three hundred. The high clay banks are lined with grass and reeds, with uninhabited bush beyond. I am in a mellow mood as we leisurely paddle

Hippo herd in the Nile, with elephants in the distance. Hippos were the greatest danger on the river, carrying out seven aggressive attacks against me and my companions.

together in close formation, following the winding channel past islands and sandbars. The day passes uneventfully until just before dusk, when my ears pick up a sound from down river that snaps me out of my contentment and fills me with dread. It is a deep basso profundo bellowing like no other sound in the animal kingdom, produced by the most life-threatening danger of the river—a hippopotamus. As we sweep around a narrow bend, my eyes widen with alarm at the frightening sight of a herd of ten hippos in midstream. "Oh! Oh!" I exclaim, "Another hippo blockade!" It has been many weeks since we have been troubled by hippos, but the appearance of the herd revives the terror I had felt during our past experiences with the monsters. Immediately alert, they grunt nervously and turn to face us. The current is too strong for us to stop or change course, and the channel too narrow to detour around them. Landing is impossible, the reeds are too thick along the right bank, and the island to our left is rank with overhanging vegetation. "Here we go again—right into the jaws of death," I mutter to myself.

One bull adds to my mounting tension by an ostentatious territorial display—throwing his massive head around and baring his deadly curved tusks in a great yawn that threatens to split his jaws. It leaves no doubt as to his intentions if we intrude into his space. We back-paddle strongly, but that only briefly delays the inevitable. We draw closer to the herd with each pounding heartbeat. It is like drifting in slow motion toward a high waterfall, helpless to stop from sweeping over and down to certain destruction. I grip the paddle so tightly that my fingernails dig into my palms. I am stiff with fear. Only one possible course of action is open to us: to go forward and pray that we can run the blockade safely.

I shoot forward on the current, steering as close as possible to the right bank. The hippos become more agitated as I approach them, ramming their broad muzzles in and out of the water with thunderous snorts of anger. I maneuver with small dips of the paddle to keep heading in the right direction with the least movement. I have the strongest feeling that a sudden move or loud sound will trigger a mass charge that will pulverize me and my kayak.

The current increases in speed as I draw abreast of the hippos nearest me. This is the break I need. It allows me to sit, virtually motionless, rigid with anxiety, until I float beyond the herd, where I come alive and paddle furiously to safe waters. I park in the reeds to nervously watch the progress of my companions. While my passage distracts the hippos, Jean seizes the chance to advance on the left side, staying close to the island. As the animals turn to stare banefully at him, his kayak grounds sickeningly on a sandbar, less than fifteen yards from two of the largest hippos. "Jean, you've got to get out of there fast, or you're done for!" Despite their menacing closeness and intensified gruntings, Jean jumps out, drags the boat free and clambers back into the cockpit. He paddles faster than I have ever seen him move before, scraping the shallow river bottom with each frantic stroke. André, hunched over his paddle, speeds close behind, in Jean's foaming wake, doing his best to escape without antagonizing the herd any further. The two pass through unscathed, without causing a charge, and immediately head over to where I am anxiously watching their break-out. André, breathless with excitement, says, "I was praying to God, the Virgin Mary and all the saints to protect me, so someone must have heard my prayers!"

Finding no landing, we paddle on after dark until the sound of drums guide us to a village of the Mandara tribe, near a settlement called Mongolla. Here we camp for the night, utterly spent after our first strenuous paddle in almost a month.

The next day we pass incredible numbers of hippos and crocodiles as we continue downstream. There are dozens of crocs of all sizes sunning on the sandy beaches. Hippos are almost constantly in view, strung out over the now-broad Nile, in one herd after another. We keep alert throughout the day for possible attacks. Jean and I pass two hippos with no trouble from either one. André, lagging behind, is forced to paddle for his life when they suddenly charge him. Every time we round a bend, the crocodiles on the banks, startled by our sudden appearance, come alive—a slithering mass of squirming bodies plunging into the water. They frequently execute spectacular dives from their sunning dens, six or eight feet above the water. Some actually perform a somersault in midair, landing with a mighty splash on their horny backs. It is thrilling to see four crocodiles, each about eight feet in length, launch themselves off a high bank and crash into the river in almost perfect unison, like a superbly trained circus act.

Later, while paddling quietly alone near the west bank, there is a commotion in a thicket on a high bank just ahead. Seconds later I look up to see a ten-foot crocodile, fang-spiked jaws slightly parted in an evil grin, bursting out of the greenery in what appears to be a ferocious ambush. It is a horrible sight when, without a moment's hesitation, the huge creature shoots off the bank, becoming airborne and coming straight at me. I nearly pass out from fright, but instantly raise my aluminum paddle in a feeble attempt to fend him off. For just a second the thought passed through my mind—*I'm going to be eaten alive!* But the heavy-bodied croc smashes explosively into the water next to me, a scant yard away. The force of his cannonball dive creates waves that wash over me and almost capsize my kayak. I am certain he is really after me when he squeezes under my kayak and lifts me a foot high out of the water. My heart speeds up like a runaway piledriver, shaking my chest forcefully with each beat. For a moment, escape is impossible because I am stuck fast, teetering precariously on top of the croc's broad back. We are separated by only a few sections of wooden framework and an eighth-of-an-inch thickness of the rubber hull. The croc can easily crush me and my bantam boat with one snap of his powerful jaws. Finally, he lowers me back into the water and moves on. As he passes beneath me I feel the hard projections of his back and tail ratcheting the soles of my bare feet as they rest on the thin hull. For weeks I have sweated out the possibility of a crocodile attack. From the beginning of our trip, they have been a common sight on land and on the surface of the river. Individual ones have even followed closely in my wake as I paddled downstream. I have watched one feeding crocodile rip chunks off a prey animal by chomping down with its huge jaws, then rapidly spin its body to tear the meat away. *What if he lunges out of the water and grabs me? Could that happen to me?* I wonder. The only thing that I can think of that might save me is to jab my thumbs into his eyes with all my strength and hope that would cause him to release me. Fortunately this drastic action is not needed, and the animal does not appear again. After the croc passes underneath the kayak, I begin paddling rapidly to get as far away as possible in case he is following me.

Far downstream, after calming down, I review what has happened. Evidently the croc, resting in the shrubbery, had been surprised by my sudden approach and had instinctively plunged into the river to escape possible danger. The timing was so close between his dive and my arrival below the bank that it appeared that he was trying to leap on top of me. If I had been just a little closer to the bank I would have been struck head-on, finding one thousand pounds of frantic crocodile on top of me, and the results would have been fatal—for me!

We arrive at a Dinka village just before sunset. A teenager named Juak welcomes us as we unload and set up camp. Having learned some English at a Protestant mission, he tells us that his people are in mourning over a double tragedy. Just a few days apart, a warrior and a young boy had been snatched away by crocodiles while they were bathing in shallow water near the village.

Men of a Dinka village escort me on a tour of their land.

Three days after leaving Juba we land at Bor, one hundred miles downstream. Though featured prominently on maps of Africa, Bor consists of a large, sprawling Dinka village and a wooden house, occupied by Major Ronald Cummings, a retired officer of the British army and the only white person living on the Nile between Juba and Bor. He is seriously ill with a virulent combination of malaria and amoebic dysentery. Judging from his emaciated appearance and fever-bright eyes, his proper place is in a hospital. But he graciously insists on getting out of bed to sit with us in his living room and ask about our experiences and plans.

Major Cummings tells us, "You chaps have been fortunate indeed to have lived through your hippo charges. The Dinka hunters hereabouts frequently have fatal run-ins with the blasted animals. Why, just yesterday, a dugout bearing six Dinka hippo hunters was smashed and sunk by a maddened hippo. Two men were killed outright, one of them nearly bitten in half. Three other Dinka drowned, and just one man survived to reach the river bank alive. This happened only five kilometers upstream, so you must have passed the spot on the way here!"

Of all the hazards we have faced to date, hippos have been by far the most life threatening. They have proved to be our deadliest menace and the greatest source of fear for us. We have run a gauntlet of belligerent hippos, intermittently, for fifteen hundred miles, during which time we have been charged on seven different occasions by aggressive bulls or females protecting their young. We have become increasingly paranoid about hippos with each new attack.*

Wind, not hippos, was our problem as we returned to the river after our visit with Major Cummings. Throughout the day we have to fight against a blustery northeaster. It whips the Nile into rough waves that bounce our kayaks up and down like rocking horses. For the first time, Jean becomes seasick. Lashed by the gale-force winds, the wild waves came close to capsizing us several times. We have our hands full every minute keeping our boats heading into the billows. If we stop paddling for just a few seconds to rest our sore muscles, our kayaks begin veering sideways, and it requires all our strength to get back on course again. It is like paddling on a storm-tossed ocean, complete with foamy whitecaps. I think of the old sailors' prayer, "Oh God, thy sea is so great and my boat is so small!"

Apart from the hard work, being tossed about on the

---

*Though fiercely protective of their young and territory, hippos are capable of gentleness and of expressing sympathy even for a creature of another species. An extraordinary demonstration of this was witnessed by a wildlife expert who photographed an adult hippopotamus actually rescuing a young female impala from a crocodile.

The antelope was about to drink at the edge of a pond when an eight-foot croc lunged from the muddy water, seized a leg and dragged her into the pool. The hippo, even though one hundred feet away, immediately charged over and chased the croc away. He nosed the injured animal ashore and stood watching as she staggered up the bank, then followed after for a closer look. The impala struggled to evade her frightening new companion as he twice gently took her head into his great mouth and then released it. The mortally wounded doe collapsed from loss of blood. The hippo began sniffing her body and licking her torn abdomen and broken leg. Finally, the impala died, but for a quarter of an hour more the hippo continued to stand over her as vultures began to appear, departing only when the fiery heat forced him to return to the pond. As the vultures converged on the body, the crocodile appeared, drove them away and reclaimed his prize.

heaving swells is exciting. My kayak is lifted high on the crest of a wave, the bottom falls out, and it smashes down into the trough with a breathtaking drop and a loud smack, only to be caught up again on the next wave. The high combers whipped up by the howling gusts become so turbulent that I am forced to head for the eastern shore, where Jean and André have already landed. I am just about to reach the beach when I'm hit with a one-two knockout punch from a pair of mischievous waves, one setting me up by tossing my prow high in the air, the other swooping in with perfect timing to blast into the kayak broadside. Over I go. Fortunately, the water is shallow, so I quickly right the shell and tow it to solid ground.

I snatch the camera case out as soon as the boat is righted so the two cameras remain dry. Then I notice that the cover on the side compartment is open and three irreplaceable lenses are missing. There is no alternative but to put my diving mask on and look for them, trusting that the blustering winds will keep the crocodiles inactive today.

Despite the endless waves, I dive repeatedly seven or eight feet without success and discouragement begins to take hold. Even this close to shore the water is cloudy from wind-driven sand, reducing visibility to less than a yard. I creep along just above the river bottom, straining to see the lenses while constantly being buffeted to and fro by the heaving waves. Then I spot a strange gleam in the murky water ahead, kick forward to investigate, and discover that the shine comes from sunlight beaming down through the shallow water and reflecting off the silver metal of the three lenses, nestled together on the sandy bottom. My search is successful!

We are so frustrated by the wind that we paddle on long after sunset, taking advantage of the calm that sets in with the cooling of the atmosphere at dusk. I live a day at a time, with no regrets from the past or fear of the future, and I enjoy each new experience. But there are moments of despair, especially after an arduous session of paddling such as exhausted us today. We made only twenty miles, and still have a whopping two thousand miles ahead of us. At times like this, our expedition seems almost *too* insurmountable a challenge.

Upon landing at Kodok, the center of the proud and

Shilluk warriors assembling to make simulated battle charges against me.

handsome Shilluk people, we find the local villagers greatly agitated over a clash with a neighboring tribe, the Dinka. Some of their herders had surprised two Dinkas in the act of rustling several head of their cattle. The Shilluks had promptly organized a punitive assault and marched to the village of the would-be thieves, where they found every able-bodied warrior armed and ready to defend their erring tribesmen. In the battle that followed, twenty-six people were speared or clubbed to death.

As I stroll around the village, mulling over the news of this shocking tragedy, I have a major scare when a procession of two dozen or more young warriors comes marching by in a cloud of dust, chanting with deep bass voices in rhythm to their steps. Leading the group are two sweaty men who prance and leap around energetically. Each man carries a long spear in his right hand and a large hippo-hide shield in his left. This is a rare opportunity to record an unusual action sequence, so I raise my camera and begin filming as they sweep past. They haven't gone far when they abruptly wheel around and head back toward me. When a few yards away they suddenly break ranks, spread out and crouch down behind their shields until they are almost hidden. Then, at a command from their leader, they spring erect, raise their spears high, stabbing them back and forth menacingly, and come rushing at me en masse in a full-blown, head-on battle charge.

I am so startled by this dramatic maneuver that I nearly drop the camera, half expecting to have my body punctured in a dozen places, but they stop short just in front of me. I begin filming again, knowing it's best to appear

Two Shilluks who participated in the charges against me with their primary weapons at ten feet in length—Africa's longest spears.

cool and not reveal any nervousness. They retreat a few steps, loudly striking their spears on their shields as they move back, then hunker down and aim a second sham attack. This time I hold steady and get it all on film. The fired-up warriors finally back off and continue on their way, leaving me to speculate on the intent of the incident. I conclude that I had been the target of an outburst of pure *esprit de corps* from a band of warriors who are aching for a fight.

LIFE GOAL #139: *Catch a Puff Adder*

Rescuing a Deadly Puff Adder

Throughout my long journey down the Nile, bird life is continually abundant and colorful, particularly in southern Sudan, which more than compensates for the monotony of constant paddling. There are birds of every conceivable color, size and shape—some flying low over the water with the wind, others perching in acacia trees near the water or congregating on sandy banks, mud bars and at the mouths of dry *wadis*. Many of them are transient, making long migrations from far-off homelands in winter-bound Europe or Asia. They vary in appearance from the stilt-legged and gawky storks to the trim little stubby-legged terns. Some birds have beaks that curve upwards, like the delicate bill of the *avocet*; others turn downwards, like that of the *hadada* ibis. The sight of each new species lifts my spirits and distracts my attention from the aches and pains of hard paddling. Imprisoned as I am on the heaving river, in my cramped kayak, fingers fused to the hot aluminum paddle and thrashing along at a snail's pace, how I envy their freedom.

During one windy February day while paddling alone in an uninhabited area of Sudan, besides beautiful birds, the only other wildlife I see is a large puff adder. This reptile kills more humans than any other snake in Africa— even more than cobras and mambas. Other venomous snakes quickly move away when they sense vibrations from the footfalls of an approaching person, but the sluggish puff adder generally remains resting in place and then strikes an unwary passerby coming too close. Though lethargic by nature, it has one of the fastest strikes of all snakes.

It is late afternoon and I am making slow progress in midstream, fighting to make headway against the assault of wind-driven waves against me, with my kayak bucking and plunging like a merry-go-round horse.

As I reach the crest of one wave I spot the snake, struggling desperately in the choppy waves, attempting to reach the western shore. It is an unexplainable mystery as to why the adder is trying to swim across the Nile, particularly at a point several hundred yards wide, and on a day with blustery wind and waves making a crossing even more difficult. I wonder what irresistible urge drives the snake to make such a suicidal effort.

I can see that it is already exhausted and will surely drown long before it can reach land. My lifelong affection for reptiles asserts itself, and since there are no villages anywhere nearby, I decide to rescue it from certain death. From the time I was eight years old until I enlisted in the air force at eighteen, I have enjoyed a succession of snake pets. These included four calm, unaggressive rattlers and a six-foot python. I was always fascinated by their grace and beauty. I have a natural urge to protect wildlife and go to the aid of any creature in distress. I carefully maneuver my kayak alongside the snake and, using both hands on my double-bladed paddle, slide one flat end underneath the heavy-bodied reptile, scoop it up out of the river and deposit it on the prow of my tossing kayak. The adder is so fatigued from its long swim that it lays without moving as I head for the shore to release it there.

Approaching the tall papyrus bordering the Nile, I begin working the paddle blade under the adder to ease it into the water, when a sudden swell lifts the prow up, throwing me off balance. At the same time a capricious wave slaps into the kayak broadside, flipping it completely over—and throwing me into the river with one of Africa's deadliest snakes! I have a feeling of cold terror as I bob to the surface, momentarily blinded by water in my eyes, and with no idea of how close I am to the adder. The snake is certainly excited and irritated by the sudden shock of being pitched into the river, and fully capable of striking and biting me even though in the water. I half expect to bump into the snake and feel its long fangs sink into my body. With the nearest hospital more than one hundred miles away, and whether the correct antivenom serum would be available is questionable, my chances of surviving a bite are slim indeed.

Fear lends speed to my reaction. I lunge out of the water, pull my legs up and sprawl face-down along the hull of the overturned kayak. For a few moments I can't see the snake anywhere, then I spy him swimming vigorously upstream, seemingly unaware of how close he is to the shore. Luckily, the waves sweep him into the green forest of flooded papyrus and then right up to the solid land beyond. The last I see of the snake, he is safely out of the river and resting quietly on the edge of the sandy bank.

I retrieve my floating paddle and ride the billowing waves astride the hull until I reach a sandbar. Here, I empty the water from my kayak, right it, and continue downstream. I am well aware that most people would think I did a foolish thing in saving the puff adder. But from my philosophy of revering all life, I feel a sense of satisfaction from enabling a fellow creature to escape death—even if it is only a snake.

LIFE GOAL #13: *Explore the Sudan*

The Anvil of the Lord

fter months of hardship and danger exploring the Nile through Uganda and southern Sudan, it is wonderful to reach Khartoum at last. This is a major achievement for us in that Khartoum, Sudan's colorful and historic capital, represents our halfway point on the Nile, roughly half the distance between the river's main source, Lake Victoria, and its mouth at the Mediterranean Sea.

We enjoy several days of cordial hospitality, offered to us by the small European colony living in Khartoum and by the friendly Sudanese officials stationed there. After the semistarvation and spartan life we have been living on the river, it is positively luxurious to be able to eat our fill of delicious food, to sleep between clean sheets in a real bed and to rest from the arduous work of paddling like galley slaves, twenty to thirty miles each day in triple-digit temperatures.

But finally, reluctant to lose our hard-won physical stamina, Jean, André and I return to our kayaks.

We thank our hosts, who had gathered on the river banks to see us off, for their generous hospitality, and then we paddle on downstream for the next leg of our adventure.

We soon enter the southern bounds of the ancient kingdom of Nubia, once called Kush by Egyptians thousands of years ago when it was a thriving crossroads of trade with Egypt. It was known as the land of Cush in the Bible. In modern times northern Sudan is largely abandoned, containing only a small population, and is one of the least known areas of Africa—completely dominated by desert.

Actually I am looking forward to traveling through this half of the Sudan. As a young boy I loved camping with my parents in several areas of California's majestic Mojave Desert. Throughout my adult years I had planned and carried out several excursions through many of the great deserts of the world, including those of Arizona, Mexico, Australia, Morocco, Afghanistan, and the Gobi of China and Inner Mongolia. Throughout the world, desert lands are neglected, abused and underrated, but I always love their unique splendor and their fascinating animal and plant life.

In spite of the punishing sun and continual hunger and thirst, I have come to love the solitude and purity of northern Sudan's virgin deserts. It is spiritually uplifting to experience this pristine world, one unblemished by urban sprawl, noise or pollution. The days flow along with no boundaries in time or space. I am constantly enveloped by sweeping, mind-expanding vistas of sky, river and land. Though they can be forbidding and harsh, the golden deserts along the Nile frequently reward me with special beauty, particularly during the fresh morning hours and in the cool dusk, often with a gorgeous sunset to enjoy before nightfall.

The star-spangled nights are a special inspiration. I have never seen our Milky Way galaxy so radiantly brilliant as in the pure desert atmosphere, far removed from the clouds of smog and the intrusive glow of cities. I come to understand how it is that many great religious leaders and prophets of old came out of the desert or developed their spiritual strength there.

Frequently during our passage through Nubia, I land and explore the ruins of palaces, fortresses and mosques on both banks, most of them built centuries ago when there were sizable settlements along the river.

Typically I am alone as I clamber around the old ruins and the only human being for many miles around. *Just me and the jackals,* I think. I see at least one resident jackal at several of these manmade relics from past centuries. These shy, attractive little canines seem to favor the ruins for setting up their dens. They always remind me of the coyotes on my Uncle Royal's big Idaho cattle ranch where I worked as a ranch hand every summer throughout my teens.

Though I am alone, for the most part, from dawn to dusk, I never experience loneliness. In fact, there are times when

I have a comforting feeling of God's presence with me.

Although I am traveling down the length of the Nile with Jean and André, it is impossible for us to stay together. Our paddling speeds and our interests are just too different. Every morning at dawn I push off in my kayak and head downriver, with my two friends following close behind. Within a few minutes we begin separating, and gradually spread out in the formation that we follow throughout the expedition, with me in the lead, André behind a mile or two, and with Jean bringing up the rear. We are like three men exploring the Nile on three separate trips. I make a camp on either bank at sundown each day and get a fire going as a beacon for my friends to steer for. After eating a light meal, we discuss what each of us has seen and experienced during the day, then collapse into our sleeping bags until the next dawn, when we continue downstream.

An hour after dawn, I am far ahead of my companions as I come upon an unusually long and violent stretch of white water. The rapid is splintered into a bewildering labyrinth of channels, sweeping over outcroppings of granite and basalt. Sitting alone on a boulder above the river, with the booming thunder of the falls assaulting my ears, I study the tricky twists and turns of the seething green flood below. My heart is pumping at high speed at the prospect of having to paddle through such a hazardous stretch. As I scan the sun-blasted landscape beyond, there is nothing in view but endless, cream-colored sand dunes, devoid of any vegetation. Suddenly, as if my mind needs relief from the sight of the barren land, a contrasting image flashes into my mind—the memory of an Edenic settlement I had visited along the Nile. It was a neat Sudanese village, above fertile green banks covered with fragrant morning glory and ivy, a thriving, irrigated vegetable garden near the adobe huts, and everything shaded by tall fruit-laden date palms where doves fluttered and cooed. The Nile flowed placidly by, its surface fragmented by a cluster of granite islets, each covered with luxuriant grass and reeds and fringed with beaches of pure white sand where ducks and geese rested. This reverie was so vivid that I found myself actually present there again, being warmly greeted by the hospitable villagers, admiring again how their attractive dark complexions created such a striking contrast with their white teeth and clothing.

As the vision faded I snapped back into the reality of still having to face the brutal white-water run. Portaging was not a possible option; I *had* to go through in my fragile kayak, but first I made a visual survey along the length of the rapids, trudging over the hot sand from its beginning to the end. I plotted a course of the safest channels to take in my pocket notebook, realizing that if I messed up and went down any of the wrong corridors, there would be only a slim chance of surviving a dunking in a cataract this long and ferocious. Then an amazing discovery took place—a "light bulb" moment, a life-changing happening. Worried about not being able to remember the correct sequence of waterways to follow, I close my eyes to determine if I can imagine the route I must take. To my surprise there appeared a picture of the rapids so clear

André and I assemble kayaks before our ill-fated trip down the Kagera River (chapter 9).

Ogone and Sabi of the Madi tribe, acting as bearers on the eight-day, 125-mile foot safari along the Nile in southern Sudan (chapter 12).

André in a papyrus jungle along Kagera.

Dinka warrior and spear used in battle and for killing hippos.

A Dinka woman with authentic jewelry.

Shilluk warriors gear up for sham battle charges against me (chapter 13).

A ten-foot crocodile dives into the Nile just in front of my kayak.

A herd of elephants greets us along the Nile.

My arrival in Egypt, fulfilling Life Goal #171, by visiting the three-thousand-year-old Temple of Abu Simbel, with its four colossal statues of Ramses II, ancient Egypt's greatest ruler, who is presumed to be the pharaoh from whom Moses freed the Hebrews.

Sphinx and Pyramid of Khafre—second largest of the three colossal pyramids at Giza, built as monumental tombs of three kings, Khufu, (Cheops), Khafre and Menkaure, to ensure preservation of their mummified bodies and to glorify their names for eternity.

Standing at the summit of the Great Pyramid, one of the wonders of the ancient and modern world (chapter 17).

Mongo, Jack Yowell and myself at the source of the Lualaba River (chapter 18).

Jack and I at spring, the fountainhead of the Congo, the world's second largest river, called Lualaba River on its upper course.

Scanning the river downstream, looking for dangerous hippos or rapids.

A mother hippo protecting her baby.

The first waterfall on the Congo, never before seen, since no one had yet
explored the first 375 miles of the river, and the banks were too overgrown
to be seen from the land.

Jack Yowell and termite nests on a hill where two explorers camped.

Running one of the 127 unknown rapids of the first 375 miles of the Lualaba.

With Jack after seventeen days in the Congo wilderness. Both of us lost fifteen pounds from the hardships of the journey.

After Jack's tragic drowning, I continued downstream by dugout. Here, I pose with nine friends of the Walengola tribe with whom I traveled for several days.

Lake Granby in the Rocky Mountains of Colorado, the source of the Colorado River.

Plane crash along the banks of the Colorado, with left wing resting in the river (chapter 19).

With a rattlesnake I caught in the Grand Canyon (chapter 20).

Capsized river-running raft in which I was thrown overboard and nearly drowned in Badger Creek Falls (chapter 21).

and realistic that I was able to stimulate my imagination further and project, on the screen of my mind, an action movie of the rapids, with me appearing and paddling my kayak down the safest passages chosen during my survey! In short, I was able to make an accurate mental rehearsal before the actual trip through! Included in the visualization was an emergency procedure to follow in case of capsizing.

With the plan firmly established in my mind, I climb into the kayak and push off into the swift torrent, and I begin zigzagging down the rock-bound corridors. Half blinded by stinging spray, my bantam boat plunging through explosions of foamy waves, it requires all my skill and concentration, paddling hard and fast, to follow the preconceived route and keep from racing down impassable channels or crashing into the gauntlet of rocks scattered over the river. Finally, after a thrilling ride, with a moment or two of raw terror, I am successful in threading my way through the maze, emerging into calm water unscathed but with the kayak about to swamp from shipping a barrel of water during the run due to the lack of the spray cover, which was ripped off and lost on the Kagera River.

The dramatic success of the mental rehearsal in helping me pass through the big cataract safely convinces me to make visualization a routine practice to use in all areas of life.*

---

*During other river expeditions involving rapids, I used the same imaging technique successfully, especially on the unexplored white-water areas of the upper Congo River, where my partner and I ran 125 rapids in our kayaks along a 350-mile hazardous stretch. Visualization has been immeasurably useful not only during danger-filled journeys, but in ordinary daily activities. Anyone can achieve meaningful benefits by developing and using this powerful technique.

After emptying the water-logged kayak, I'm back on the river again and it's still only 9:00 A.M. On this traumatically torrid and unforgettable day, I experience a dramatic reminder of how overpowering and dangerous the desert can be, even just a short distance from the life-sustaining Nile.

A few miles along, I beach my kayak on the narrow shore of the west bank. My view of the desert has been cut off by a towering wall of sand that rises from the river's edge to a height of about twenty feet. In addition to exercising my legs, numb after sitting mostly in the kayak since dawn, I want to inspect the desert beyond, to see if there are any ruins nearby or anything that is worth investigating. When I reach the top of the bank, I inspect the area with my binoculars and immediately spot a rugged formation of sandstone about a mile away. Since it was only about ninety-five degrees (cool for Nubia!), I decide to make a quick march over to the outcroppings to explore them, in hopes of finding ruins of some kind or ancient petroglyphs inscribed on the walls.

A few days earlier a Sudanese friend had led me on a hike out in the desert to some bare rock hills to show me a bonanza of well-preserved ancient etchings. They represented a long procession of travelers who had passed through here over the ages. The petroglyphs included primitive drawings of lions, giraffes, ostriches, buffalo and antelope. They had been carved by Stone Age hunters at a time when Nubia, part of the eastern Sahara, had a moist climate, was forested and inhabited by animals now found only hundreds of miles farther south. There were also ancient Egyptian hieroglyphics, signatures in Greek, Meroetic inscriptions and Christian Jerusalem crosses. The most recent inscriptions were in Arabic, dating from the 16th century.

Dressed in my usual khaki shirt and shorts, wearing my broad-brimmed Australian bush hat and carrying only my canvas canteen, I begin hiking over one of the least inhabited and most incandescently hot expanses of the vast Sahara Desert. The world's largest desert, the Sahara extends from the Nile all the way across Africa to the Atlantic Ocean. Long ago, Arab caravaneers called it "The Anvil of the Lord," because they believed it was a creation of Allah, designed to forge invincible character in those who chose to travel in this formidable desert.

By the time I trudge across the scorching sand to the outcroppings, my head feels like it's on the verge of being incinerated by the merciless sun. I gradually revive after resting for an hour in the shade of the rocks and taking several swigs from my canteen.

Though I carefully search around the formations, I can't find any evidence that humans have ever visited here before me, as any record of this probably has been obliterated by powerful sandstorms over the ages. There are only splashes of dried guano staining the rocks, from vultures roosting on them. After ravenously guzzling the last of my water, I begin heading back to my kayak. A sudden twinge of alarm creeps over me as I scan the blazing desert and realize how far I have to trek to reach the river.

The Nile isn't visible anywhere, as it is deep in its channel, well below the banks. Nevertheless, I head eastward, knowing that I have to hit it eventually. It isn't long before rivulets of hot, salty sweat begin dripping down from under my heavy felt hat, immediately drying to a thin crust on my face. It has been several hours since I left the river, and now the brutal sun is high in the cloudless sky. After only a few minutes, I begin feeling weak and nauseous from heat exhaustion. It feels as if I am inflaming my lungs with every breath. My khaki shirt is so hot and uncomfortable that I want to rip it off, but realize that would only accelerate my deterioration. Though I am wearing thick crepe-soled safari shoes, the bottoms of my feet burn painfully from the hot sand as I shuffle along.

I stop and rest for a few moments, bent over with my hands on my knees, but when I stand up and open my eyes, nothing appears the same. I can still see the sandstone formations in the distance, shimmering through the heat haze as if ablaze, but they seem to be in the wrong location.

Now completely disoriented and unsure of which way to head, I set off again, staggering along for what seems much farther than where the Nile should be and feeling increasingly feeble. It seems incredible that the great river can be so tantalizingly close and yet so well concealed that I can't find it. Within another half hour I notice that I have stopped sweating, which means that my metabolism is shutting down to allow my body to absorb every last ounce of internal moisture. The force of the sun's rays doubles from being reflected off all the glaring surfaces. It is brain-curdlingly hot! So hot, in fact, that I can't even spit! On the river, whenever I become overheated I lean over the side of my kayak, fill my large hat with water and plop it on top of my head for a brief but refreshing shower. On super-hot afternoons, I occasionally jump overboard and swim along, towing my kayak by the prow rope, to combine surviving the heat with exercise for my legs. But here on the desert there is no way to relieve my torment from the sun. I am furious with myself for being in this deadly predicament. By leaving the river to make the dangerous hike out on the desert, I have recklessly ignored the usual instinctive caution that had saved me from serious harm in the past. I haven't taken a sufficient water supply with me, and though having been acclimated to heat for several weeks, I have underestimated the time it requires to reach the outcroppings and then return to the river.

I am desperately confused and lost—swallowed in an infinity of silent, sun-scorched desert, stretching ahead to every horizon and marked only by custard-yellow sand dunes and wind-scoured hard-pan rock. There isn't a living thing in sight, not a camel, or a vulture or even a sprig of vegetation. The only movement is that of a "dust-devil," a sandy whirlwind some Moslems believe is the manifestation of a supernatural spirit they call a "Jinni."

My throat feels like dry parchment and my tongue becomes swollen. I am madly thirsty and now suffering from the severe dehydration created by the sizzling heat that envelops me like a fiery fog. It doesn't help my condition when I suddenly recall the horrible desert disaster that had occurred in the previous century in which a caravan of two thousand men and eighteen hundred camels died of thirst in the Sahara, because the wells and oases along their line of march had dried up. I feel an urgent sense of panic as it becomes inescapably obvious that I am going to die unless I can reach water within the next few minutes. My head throbs from a heavy migraine, adding to the misery of a raging fever and blurring vision as my heat exhaustion intensifies into a classic case of heatstroke. I have never felt so sick or weak before in my life. I imagine my friends finding my heat-cured, mummified body lying on the desert, only a short distance from my beached kayak. But as I stand, trying to get my bearings, I hear the plaintive cry of a bird—to my ears the most glorious sound imaginable— the first sign of life of the entire day. It is a little brown and white plover which appears, providentially, at this critical time, for a brief moment. It is flying above a sand dune on my left, only one hundred feet away, then dips down behind it and is gone.

It takes a few seconds for my feverish brain to process the importance of this sighting, but finally it hits me! The plover is not a desert dweller; it is a bird that is always associated with water and spends its life along seashores, lakes and *rivers!*

In a burst of newfound energy I stumble on toward the dune, crawl up the loose sand to the top where I behold the thrilling sight of the pale, green Nile flowing peacefully along directly below me. The last of my strength has been exhausted in struggling up the frustrating, slippery sand of the hill, so all I can do is collapse in a limp heap, my hat tightly clutched to me, and slide, tumble and roll, nonstop, with tremendous relief, down the steep slope, right out into the river! I half expect to see steam rise from my burning body as I plunge headfirst into the cool water. I begin drinking voraciously until a sudden sharp cramp warns that I have to slow down to not upset my parched stomach with too much—too fast. But never has water tasted so delicious!

After blissfully drinking to satisfaction (while keeping an eye out for lurking crocodiles), I feel my dangerously high temperature gradually cool down. I rest in the shallows, immersed up to my neck in the soothing water, unwilling to sit up. If there were a hospital available I would check myself in to recuperate for a day or two. Since this is not possible, there is nothing to do but move on.

Physically, I am so drained of strength that it is difficult to get back on my feet. When I stand up I have the strange sensation of my feet being anchored in the sand. I summon the energy to limp over to the kayak, feeling on the verge of passing out and tortured by the pounding headache that is aggravated by each step.

Launching the kayak leaves me breathless and unable to do anything more than drift along on the gentle current. Gradually, I am able to begin paddling in slow but steady strokes, leaving the fiery region where I have come so close to dying. Though my body is in a deplorable condition, emotionally I am filled with a glowing sense of happiness over my survival from what could have been a fatal case of heatstroke. I paddle away, silently blessing my winged rescuer, the little plover, which had so mysteriously appeared at just the right moment to lead me away from certain death and toward deliverance.

LIFE GOAL #177: *Visit Egypt*

Ambushed by Egyptian River Pirates

It is evening, Jean and André have not yet caught up with me here in this isolated desert region of Egypt. I decide to stop paddling and spend the night at a small village just ahead. After landing and checking it out, I find it so squalid and the peasant farmers, or *fellahin*, so sullen and rough-looking that I continue downriver.

A mile or two farther on, the sight of a palm-branch hut above the shoreline, with a cheery campfire in front of it, looks promising. I pull in and land, hoping to spend the night here. After covering half the distance to the hut, trudging up the sloping sandbank, I am caught completely off guard when two large mongrel dogs streak out of the darkness toward me.

They appear like demons incarnate, with their eyes and bared fangs gleaming in the firelight, their emaciated bodies reeking of the cadaverous stench of death. Circling, they edge in close and savagely attack me. With no weapon to defend myself, I whip out my red bandana and, by snapping it at their noses, am able to briefly hold them off. The large cloth is soon ripped out of my hands and torn to shreds. All I can do now is vigorously kick at the lunging beasts, receiving several bites on my ankles and legs from the effort. They attack from both sides, their ferocious determination to seize me emphasized by their ominous silence.

I had been warned that the vicious, half-wild village dogs of Egypt can be as predatory as hyenas and just as dangerous. They are not treated as valued pets, but are mostly ignored to survive on their own, unloved and only sporadically fed. They have a notorious reputation for killing and devouring strangers traveling alone in the countryside. Many village curs are easily intimidated as a result of continual mistreatment. Judging by the violence of their attack, these dogs are so emboldened by ravenous hunger and my lack of a weapon that they regard me as prey—an easy source of fresh meat to fill their shrunken bellies. I know if they succeed in dragging me down, I'm finished.

The fellah, a thin young man with a short beard, finally comes rushing over to rescue me, and with heavy blows of his staff beats the crazed animals back. The farmer, very distressed by the attack on me by his dogs, apologizes in a gush of Arabic.

When the dogs spring at me again, even while I am sitting with their master in front of the campfire, I know it's best to get out of there *fast*! The beasts don't give up though. They follow close behind me, all the way back to the kayak, snapping at my feet and snarling in frustration, held back only by the stout staff of my flustered host. This was one of the few times in my life when I haven't been able to calm down and make friends with strange dogs—even aggressive ones.

The wind is strong and blustery as I paddle downstream with no village in sight. I stop at a beach on the west bank and apply antibiotic ointment to the dog bites, fervently hoping neither animal is rabid. For warmth in the chilly desert air I put on extra clothing and bed down on the latticed bottom of the kayak—much like sleeping on a woodpile.

I haven't been asleep more than an hour when the quietness of the night is fractured by the blast of a rifle shot. The explosion springs me upright and wide awake. I'm unable to see the shooter anywhere, though the gun has been fired no more than fifty yards away, and it is a moonlit night. It seems likely that my kayak, so starkly white in the bright moonlight, has been the target of the mysterious sniper. I launch forth on the Nile again, rushing to escape from so hostile an area, paddling for an hour before pulling in at a sandy shore where I sleep until dawn.

I have no idea when I awaken on the deserted beach

that I am about to experience a life-or-death ordeal. I set off downstream to find a village and to wait for Jean and André. High palisades parallel the river on the east bank, and stark, flat desert lay on the west. At about 9 A.M., as I fight to make headway against the stiff wind, I am hailed by two men on the right bank, who call out to me to stop and visit with them. They are a sinister-looking pair, so I merely return their greeting and continue on my way.

They persist, however, running along the bank and shouting after me to come over to them. I begin speeding up, edging toward the middle of the river, even though it is rougher there, whereupon the two men run ahead of me downstream to a rowboat *felucca*, where four other hoodlums join them. The six begin to row frantically, three on an oar, to reach me. Only by paddling as fast as I can do I manage to keep ahead of them.

While the chase is on, I notice men gathering on both banks, several carrying rifles and clubs and all bearing long staffs. A short time later other feluccas loaded with men begin a campaign to bottle me up and intercept me.

Altogether five boats—two feluccas under sail and three rowboats—take part in the pursuit, and I am hard put to elude them. Just as it seems that I am escaping them, a man on the left bank wades knee-deep into the river, levels his rifle and fires. The bullet strikes the water a few feet in front of the kayak.

Immediately I become the target of all the outlaws with rifles, and they bang away. Two of the bullets nearly part my hair; their eerie whine as they streak over chills me. I scrunch down in the boat as best I can to offer as small a target as possible, then paddle as if Satan himself is after me.

For once I find myself blessing the incessant wind instead of cursing it. The waves it creates keep me bobbing like a cork, making me a difficult target.

The gunfire sounds exceptionally loud, although most of the snipers are one or two hundred yards away. One blast, apparently aimed at my head, sounds full in my ear, causing it to ring and throb. My pulse rate must be setting a new high when the bullets begin kicking up spray around the kayak. It seems such a paradox that I find myself in mortal danger, fleeing for my life, as our expedition is nearing completion and, we think, all the worst danger is behind us. But there I am, flailing the wind-tossed water with the last of my strength—bullets zinging all around and the blasts of the guns and the shouts and curses of the bandits resounding in my ears.

Most of them give up the chase after I have paddled out of range of their guns, but a few, six or seven, continue to run along the left bank. It takes me a few minutes to realize what they are trying to do. The Nile is so low at this time of the year that many sandbars and small islands that normally are submerged under several feet of water during the flood season are now exposed. The bandits are running downstream a couple of miles to a point where the river channel is narrowed by a big sandbar. Obviously they hoped to catch me as I pass through this narrow gap, which they can easily wade across.

My back and arms are throbbing with fatigue from the terrific exertion I have already undergone; but when I see this new danger, I forget my exhaustion and paddle as never before to beat them to the slender passage. Once through, I know I will be safe because the river beyond balloons out to more than three hundred yards wide.

It's a nip-and-tuck race, with the wind holding me back. As the river narrows, I am forced nearer and nearer to my assailants, who take advantage of their good luck by hurling large rocks at me. Fortunately, none of them has a rifle, but some of the rocks strike my boat although they don't do any real damage because the range is still too far.

Struggling against the wind with my attackers close behind, I hear them whooping like Apaches on the warpath as I shoot through the narrow channel just before they reach it. They splash and shout in rage at losing me. I experience a glowing sense of victory as I flaunt my successful escape by turning around in my kayak and giving them the international gesture of defiance and contempt—the one finger salute.

At the next bend in the river I am grateful to see a small village on the left bank and hurry over to see if there is a *khaffir* to whom I can report the attack and secure protection for Jean and André, who have yet to pass that section of the river. The first person I meet upon landing is a rifle-carrying Egyptian with two bandoleers of bullets crisscrossing his chest! But he is peaceful and leads me to the home of the village *omdah* without saying a word.

I have a long wait before the mayor, dopey and heavy-eyed from slumbering, makes an appearance. I explain the details of my ambush and ask what can be done to protect my comrades. He is sympathetic but philosophical about my harrowing experience. His first comment is, *"Malish,"* meaning roughly, "It is fate," or "Don't worry, it could've been worse." (*"Malish"* is one of the favorite expressions of the fellahin and exemplifies their fatalistic belief that all the problems of life, major and minor, are due to the indisputable will of Allah.) For a long time he hems and haws before finally dispatching some of his armed men upstream to help Jean and André get through safely. Then there is nothing I can do but sweat out the arrival of my friends.

They reach the village two hours later, seething with rage over having experienced a repetition of what had happened to me. Feluccas intercepted them, they were chased on foot and by boat, they were shot at, rocks were thrown at them, and they barely eluded their attackers. The guards sent by the omdah never showed up—no doubt unwilling to risk their lives in a showdown with the pirates.*

---

*During a press conference in Cairo two weeks later, we described this attack to the assembled journalists. Our description of this dangerous experience appeared in several Arabic newspapers and aroused prompt action from government authorities. This resulted in a posse of two hundred Egyptian soldiers being dispatched to upper Egypt to hunt down the outlaws, who, faced with this formidable force, quickly surrendered after only a brief skirmish. Later we learned that this same gang had been preying on riverboats for several months. They had been intercepting feluccas periodically, hijacking their cargoes and robbing the crews. Evidently, there had been no serious effort to arrest the pirates until our description of their attempt to kill and rob us provided the catalyst for the successful operation against them.

Standing between two of the four gigantic sixty-six-foot tall statues of the cliff temple of Ramses II at Abu Simbel in Upper Egypt, carved from tawny sandstone, 1,300 years before Christ, and still considered one of the most monumental achievements of all architectural wonders. An awestruck French scholar once wrote, "Try to imagine the cathedral of Notre Dame carved out of a single block of stone!"

Visiting the Temple of Elsibu in Upper Egypt. (Life goal #172)

LIFE GOALS #178, #183, #120 & #179:

Visit Cairo, Visit Sphinx, Climb Pyramid of Cheops and Visit Cairo Museum

Attack of the Fellahin

We enjoy two activity-filled weeks in Cairo, Egypt's capital and Africa's largest metropolis. It was founded one thousand years ago, making it one of the world's oldest active cities. During our hectic visit here I fulfill several teenage goals, including climbing to the top of the stupendous 4,600-year-old Great Pyramid of Cheops (Khufu). Ever since its construction right up to modern times, it has been considered one of the seven wonders of the world. This manmade marvel was built with an incredible 2.3 million limestone blocks, each weighing two and-one-half tons, and stacked up in 210 layers to a height equivalent to a forty-story building. It is a masterwork of human engineering and design!

While standing on the narrow summit of the Great

Pyramid, I can see, in one sweeping panorama, everything characteristic of this extraordinary country of Egypt: the smoldering, beige-colored desert; the dark-green lifeline of the Nile; and the fertile farms bordering the river, shaded by graceful palms, presenting an attractive contrast to Cairo's dusty urban sprawl. Below me, near the base of the Pyramid, rests the colossal figure of the famous Sphinx, sculptured out of natural rock, with the head of a man and the body of a lion.

This torrid July morning finds us back in our kayaks, heading downstream on the Nile, only 160 miles from our final destination, the blue Mediterranean Sea. Sixteen miles north of Cairo, we encounter the Mohammed Ali barrage and are forced to detour thirty miles down the Beheira Canal due to the low water level of the Nile below the dam.

We are pleased to find a steady current flowing in the Beheira, even though the stream is only eighty to one hundred feet wide. Beyond the barrage the Nile divides into two main channels, one flowing 145 miles northwest to Rosetta, and the other flowing northeast for 150 miles to Damietta.

Traveling down the Beheira, en route to Rosetta, gives us an excellent opportunity to observe the flow of daily activities of the Nile Delta villagers. We paddle quietly down the canal within a short distance of their dwellings and cultivations, often gliding past fellahin without their being aware of our presence. However, whenever I approach too near the women working along the banks, they scatter like a covey of frightened quail.

The Egyptian Delta is one of the most densely populated and fertile regions of the world, where every acre of land is utilized. The land is green with fields of cotton, durra, corn, beans, melons, rice and okra. Small, compact adobe villages border the canal and are adorned with luxuriant banana groves, conifers, willows and colorful displays of bougainvillea.

At a large farm estate, the gruff overseer offers us a room for the night and even provides us with a supper of hard-boiled eggs, pita bread and three bottles of soda. But he keeps us awake for hours by bounding into our room to open or close the window or start up another conversation. I have to restrain myself from clouting him when he comes in at 1 A.M. and wakes me up by nudging me with his rifle butt to ask me what time it is.

We are awakened at dawn by the obnoxious overseer, so we are off to an early start. We have a few moments of concern when, after I have filmed our passage through a lock in the next barrage, several policemen challenge me for photographing "an installation of strategic importance." Before I can produce my government pass and document of permission to photograph in Egypt, a crowd gathers around me, muttering curses and threats against me. I should realize our troubles are not over even after I have identified myself.

About an hour later I begin filming a fleet of high-masted, dutch-shoe-shaped feluccas that are sailing toward me upstream. When some peasants see me, a bearded foreigner in a strange boat pointing a camera in the direction of a bridge (quite by accident), they evidently conclude that I am a particularly reckless Israeli spy on a mission of espionage. The fellahin quickly work themselves into a state of hysterical agitation and begin chasing after me along the bank in an ever-growing, loudly jabbering mob. I don't quite understand what the ruckus is about, but I know we'd better paddle out of the area as fast as possible. I shout to Jean and André behind me to speed up and look out for trouble.

We haven't paddled far when the crowd begins bombarding us with big, hard chunks of adobe clay. Men who only a few moments before had greeted me in the most friendly manner are now lusting for my blood—earnestly doing their best to bash me with grapefruit-sized clods. The violent force with which they are thrown leaves little doubt in my mind of what my chances are of surviving a direct hit on the head.

Several other men, seeing their countrymen attacking a stranger, immediately join in and begin pelting me from the other bank with anything they can lay their hands on. If any of them have firearms, it is the end of us.

I chance a quick glance behind me to see how Jean and André are making out and am dismayed to see that they have landed and are in the custody of a mob of enraged fellahin. I am rapidly being overcome by the fusillade of clods, so I have no alternative but to surrender and take a chance on the consequences.

Even after I have capitulated, the crowd is in such a frenzy that they continue pitching sticks and clods at me. Miraculously, I come through the intense bombardment with only bruises on my arms and shoulder, but the kayak is struck several times.

About this time I start feeling somewhat belligerent

myself. I furiously paddle to shore, jump out of my boat onto the bank, grab the two attackers nearest me by their necks and begin to shake some sense into them. Everyone begins to calm down, but I have a few tense moments when one of the peasants climbs onto my kayak and orders me to paddle upstream, with him perched on the prow. I know he can't stay there a minute before the boat will capsize. Fortunately, his attention is diverted, and instead he requisitions my two cameras and struts down the dusty road next to the river toward the little village of Kaaf Shubra where Jean and André have been taken into custody. With the mob following at his heels, I follow in my kayak, ready to explode with rage.

I tie up my boat, then join my comrades, who are trying to show their passports to several khaffirs but are being so jostled by the rabble that they can barely stand. There are more than three hundred people in the village, all of them crowding around us, shoving and cursing, and every one of them hostile to us. Somehow the rumor has swept through the mob that we are not Israelis but Englishmen, whom they hate almost as much as Jews.

The situation is getting out of hand. It seems we might be murdered on the spot. I demand that we be taken to the omdah immediately, whereupon we are herded down a winding narrow alley in a cloud of dust to the dwelling of the village chief. The mob bustles along all around us, shouting, reviling and even spitting at us. I feel like we have become prisoners of a bloodthirsty lynch mob and are being led to execution.

The omdah, who meets us in front of his ramshackle

Arab feluccas in the Nile Delta. This photograph precipitated an attack by 300 Egyptian fellahin (peasant farmers) who mistook me and my two French companions for being Israeli spies. The canal locks in the distance were considered "an installation of strategic importance" and therefore photography was not allowed.

hovel, proves to be a doddering old man, completely confused by our appearance. We present the two documents from government officials in Cairo identifying us and authorizing us to photograph. The papers written in flowing Arabic and affixed with important-looking stamps, seals and signatures are supposed to protect us from precisely this kind of embroilment. All he has to do is check these papers, see that they are satisfactory, order our release and allow us to continue on our way.

But from the way the ancient omdah and others in the mob turn the documents in all directions it is obvious that no one there can read them. He decides we should be taken to a police post two miles away. No amount of reasoning with him alters his decision, and since we are outnumbered a hundred to one, we have to fight down our anger and start marching to the post.

As we start to leave, we are startled to see several khaffirs brutally lash out with their long staves to clear a path through the masses of villagers crowding around us.

When one young fellah protests the whippings, he receives a vicious slap across the face, which makes him cry. Another man—incensed when a khaffir strikes his boy across the back, raising a long red welt—grabs the guard's arm to restrain him. He receives a hard kick and a punch to his head from the arrogant guard.

I think for a minute that a fight will start between the villagers and the khaffirs, but the latter beat or kick everyone who gets in their way and in that manner open the way for us to leave.

It is a long, hot walk to the little police station, but we finally arrive, with the cocky "hero" who has captured me leading the way astride a white donkey. I try several times to rescue my cameras from the grubby roughneck to protect them from the clouds of dust and sand kicked up by our feet—but each time I make the attempt, he jerks them so savagely from my grasp that, rather than jeopardize the precious equipment, I let him have his way.

We are held prisoners for more than four hours in the squalor of the vermin-infested jail until a police lieutenant arrives from a neighboring town. He is about the twentieth person to examine our passports and other official papers, and like all the others he is completely perplexed as to what to do. So he loads us in his pickup truck and drives to the commandant of police at the large town of Minouf to decide our case.

Fortunately, the commandant, Medhat el Morrass, can speak English and, as he puts it, has "followed the expedition with envy from the beginning." He apologizes profusely for the attack and tries to make amends by extending an invitation to have supper and spend the night at his home. Since it is too late to continue our journey, we accept. But first we have him drive us back to our kayaks at the small village to make certain a khaffir is stationed to guard them during our absence.

When we return to Minouf, Medhat drives us on a tour of the city, introduces us at his social club, and provides us with an excellent supper and comfortable beds. His kind hospitality soon soothes our anger at our harsh treatment from the mob, and I begin to realize we are lucky to have escaped with our lives and without even any serious injury. In each of our worst experiences on the Nile—as in the calamities of life—we always find *something* to be grateful for.

As we are leaving this morning our generous host informs us, "I'm arranging for your protection along the way to Rosetta, so that you may finish your travels in peace"—a masterpiece of understatement, as we soon discover.

We find the kayaks undisturbed, with two guards

Mounted on handsome Arabian stallions, three guards of a total twenty-four policemen who served as a protective escort during the last one hundred miles of the expedition down the world's longest river, the 4,220-mile Nile.

watching over them, and a remarkably subdued crowd lining the banks waiting for us. They humbly step aside as we thread our way past them to our boats; then they respectfully wave us on our way as we load up and shove off. "Why, they seem genuinely sorry that they tried to kill us!" I say to André. As we move downstream, a green police pickup, with two lieutenants in the cab and six policemen crowded together in back, appears along the dirt road paralleling the river. All day they stick close to us, at times racing ahead to alert villages of our arrival and generally keeping everything under control by their presence. The villagers we pass are so awed by our police escort and our strange boats that they stand transfixed at the sight of us. Some of them even allow us to approach and photograph them with no reaction other than smiles of bewilderment. After a few hours of travel, the truck is replaced by three khaki-clad policemen wearing red fezes, mounted on three magnificent Arabian stallions and carrying rifles in their saddle holsters. Every few miles a fresh team takes over to continue the escort.

During our four-day trip we are in "protective custody" —watched over continually by a total of twenty-four

Fellahin women doing their laundry and bathing along the shores of the Beheira Canal. Note the mounted policemen on the banks.

police guards riding their handsome thoroughbreds and ready to prevent any intrusion on our "peace." After traveling thousands of miles through so many of Africa's wildest and most danger-filled wildernesses, virtually unarmed and completely on our own, I can't help but find it highly amusing and more than ironic that now, back in civilization, we require armed guardians to ensure our safety during the last hundred miles of our expedition down the world's longest river, the 4,220-mile Nile.

LIFE GOALS #3 & #9: Explore the Congo River and Study Tribal Cultures in the Congo

Exploring the Upper Congo—The Lualaba

Number three on my list of life goals was to explore the entire length of the tremendous Congo River in central Africa. This is the world's second biggest river—only the Amazon is larger. No one before us had ever seen or traveled its twenty-seven-hundred-mile length.

My partner on the Congo was an exceptional man, Jack Yowell, a thirty-six-year-old white African from Nairobi, the capital city of Kenya. He had been raised in Kenya, largely by a loving African nanny of the Kikuyu tribe. Jack felt a compassionate respect for African villagers and a love of nature and wildlife identical to my own. We were true kindred spirits. We spent an incredible six weeks together, most of the time exploring the 375 wild first miles of the Congo, from its tiny headspring, in the country of Congo (Kinshasa) near the border of Zambia, to the beginning of steamer navigation. It was our intention to paddle kayaks and dugouts the length of the Congo, from its source to its mouth, all the way to the Atlantic Ocean.

Jack and I flew from Nairobi to the small town of Lubumbashi, the capital of Shaba Province in the country of Congo (Kinshasa), to make final preparations for our ambitious river project. We devoted eight busy days to interrogating government officials and other authorities to gather firsthand information about the river. Also, we purchased equipment, maps and food supplies for the expedition. At the end of our visit, however, we still had not solved two critical problems, one, determining the exact location of the source of the Congo and, two, arranging transportation to reach it. Though the officials we questioned gave us some details about the river, none of those we met had ever seen the source, nor did they know anyone who had reached it. They could only tell us what we already knew, that "It is somewhere in southeast Shaba Province."

Our discouragement over this setback is replaced with instantaneous elation when, through a series of introductions we meet Mongo, a uniformed *askari*, or military policeman, who had grown up in a village of the Bakaonde tribe, only a few miles from the source. He had actually been taken to see the source by his father when he was a boy!

Mongo's commander shows us on a territorial map a faint line representing a narrow dirt road that passes close by the fabled source. After some discussion, Jack and I are overwhelmed when the official says, "I've always wanted to see the source for myself, but have just been too busy. However, I'm going to assign Mongo to personally escort you there, and you can ride in one of my new Land Rovers!" Great news indeed!

We begin the trip early the next morning in the heavily loaded Rover, with Shoki, one of the commander's aides, at the wheel. We drive southwest for one hundred miles toward the border of Zambia at only twenty-five miles per hour, bumping over a single lane, pot-holed dirt track through a continuous wilderness of bush and forest.

During the late afternoon we pass Mongo's village, one of the few settlements in this thinly populated region. We continue ten miles farther, then at Mongo's direction, Shoki pulls over and parks.

We jump out and begin following Mongo, at a fast pace, through the woods and into the depths of a dense thicket. When he stops, Mongo points to a momentous sight, one that will mark the official starting point of our expedition.

In the dim light we can barely make out a spring of clear water, gently oozing out of the ground—the first appearance of the great Congo! (It is also called the Lualaba, which is considered the upper Congo River.)

Though the Congo is an expansive seven miles wide at its mouth, where it flows into the Atlantic Ocean, its head water is this humble spring, only a few inches deep and one or two feet wide.

"Not enough water to float a baby crocodile," I observe to Jack.

"Right, and not a very impressive beginning for the second biggest river on Earth, is it?" he replies.

After taking flash photos of the spring, we return to the Rover and continue down a side track to the village of Kikuyu. Enroute, our vehicle bogs down as we try to splash through a marshy area, and we are forced to spend the night in the woods. When Mongo discovers fresh lion tracks along the edge of the water, we feel nervous about camping outside. But we sleep close to a large campfire, which is kept going all night with dead branches, and have no problems from any kind of wildlife.

Just after dawn, Mongo volunteers to hike four miles to the village. He returns before noon with three men eager to assist us in extricating the Rover. Our combined muscle power, plus a solid foundation of branches under the tires, gets us underway again within an hour.

Shoki, driving in low gear with intense concentration, has difficulty following the narrow "cow path" because it is so overgrown with tall marshgrass and bushes that it suffers from lack of use. When we arrive at the village at the end of the track, the entire population, consisting of about forty men, women and *totos* (children), is lined up to welcome us. Everyone is bursting with excitement over our unexpected visit, laughing gleefully and clapping their hands in welcome. This happy delegation is headed by the man the village was named after, Chief Kikuyu, a lean six-footer with a solemn dignity, wearing a white pith helmet and white khaki uniform. After a pleasant get-acquainted visit, and with the friendly cooperation of the chief, we have arranged for the Kikuyu men to accompany us to the river, and we are ready to leave.

We set out over a footpath for the Lualaba, five miles from the village, with nine of the strongest men bearing our disassembled mummy-shaped kayaks and our baggage balanced on their heads. Seven other Kikuyus follow in the rear, all eighteen of us trekking along in a colorful African foot safari. The barefooted Africans carry on an animated, nonstop talkfest about this unexpected adventure that has come into their lives.

Though we are ten or eleven miles from the headspring, we are disappointed to find that the Lualaba is still only the size of a large creek. The Africans assure us that the stream develops rapidly, and that we will have no trouble traveling downstream in our small boats. Under the watchful scrutiny of our companions, we lay out all of our equipment on the bank next to the water. Next, we proceed to open and assemble the two kayaks, each one consisting of a dozen sections fitted tightly together to form a skeletal frame, which we insert into the canvas and rubber outer envelope. Each completed kayak is fifteen feet in length and fifty-five pounds in weight. I had chosen to use kayaks on the upper Congo because they had proven to be so ideal traveling down the Nile River. They are lightweight, compact, maneuverable and nonpolluting. But the small boats are also disturbingly fragile, constructed not of a tough material like fiberglass or of neoprene rubber, but of slender sections of hickory wood. This framework is enclosed within a canvas and rubber skin only one-eighth of an inch thick and vulnerable to damage from colliding with rocks or submerged logs or snags—or the jaws of a crocodile.

As darkness approaches, we pay off our bearers for

their indispensable services, giving each one triple the amount we had originally agreed on. They head back to Kikuyu, chanting with happiness over their unantici-pated bonus. We snack on a light supper, then settle down for the night. We knew the altitude at Kikuyu is forty-five hundred feet above sea level, but Jack and I, being in the heart of Africa, are unpleasantly surprised at how unbelievably cold it becomes during the night as we shiver in our sleeping bags. Even with extra clothing, we are chilled to the marrow.

Just after noon the next day, we finish loading all of our gear in every nook and cranny of the limited spaces of our boats and shove off for the big adventure. There are the

I use my machete to bushwhack a passage through an almost impene-trable jungle of trees and shrubbery enveloping the Lualaba River for at least sixty miles.

usual contrasting feelings of excitement and anxiety, aroused whenever I was about to cut off all ties with the familiar world and head into the unknown. Only two hundred yards ahead, with me in the lead, we slam into a flooded jungle of trees and huge bushes growing out of the shallow stream. The tangle of interlacing branches and shrubbery form a dense barricade that stops us cold. "Jack, there's more vegetation here than water."

"What'll we do now?" responds Jack. "We can't very well get out and walk, can we?"

The only way we can penetrate this obstacle is for me to pull out the large *panga*, or machete, I had purchased in Nairobi and begin slashing a passage just wide enough for our kayaks to squeeze through.

We are able to struggle past this barrier by pulling ourselves through my machete cuts, hand over hand, limb to limb, scooting our kayaks forward at the same time. Unfortunately, the channel opens for only a short distance, then becomes clogged again by almost impenetrable growth, which renders our paddles useless.

As Jack and I fight our way through the cleared passageways, we loosed a shower of spiders, ticks, chiggers, stinging ants and biting beetles on us, and even worse, stirred up hordes of hungry, bloodsucking, anopheles mosquitoes—the kind that transmit malaria. Our sweaty presences also attract those little devils of the bush—tsetse flies, carriers of the deadly disease called sleeping sickness. Their deep bites draw blood and make us flinch in pain from what feels like hot needles being jabbed into us. The aggressive insects feast on every exposed area of

Jack Yowell hung up in a tree growing out of Lualaba.

our bodies, and several even invade our ears, nostrils and eyes. It is difficult defending ourselves against their attacks, hemmed in as we are by the suffocating shrubbery. It is sheer misery when several tsetses find their way inside our kayaks and begin feasting on our unprotected legs beyond our reach. I nearly go berserk when a large ant penetrates far into my right ear and remains there, inaccessible and unhurried, for several interminable minutes before backing out.

Because the Lualaba is in its infancy stage, I believed that the dense thickets enveloping the stream would be only a temporary frustration. It seemed logical, based on my experience with other water courses I had explored, that as we travel downriver the main channel would broaden and deepen, and the vegetation would retreat, allowing us to paddle freely. But that is not to be.

For hours, we have to contend with the maddening

Jack Yowell follows me through the dense undergrowth.

situation of short stretches of open water, then the exasperating natural arboretum for me to hack through until I am groggy with fatigue. Jack wants to alternate with me in the job of clearing a passage, but I decline his offer with thanks since I am more experienced in handling a machete and a skittish kayak.

By dark, we have traveled less than four miles and my arms are hurting from all the heavy labor of bushwhacking.

We make camp on the eastern bank in the midst of a field covered with orange-colored, stalagmite-shaped termite nests. Another frigid night, but we wrap ourselves in our large bath towels and the canvas spray covers from our kayaks to help keep out the cold. I awake around midnight to find myself on the hard-packed ground. Upon investigation I discover that termites have eaten two holes in my air mattress, damaging it beyond repair. This little accident means I will be sleeping on the ground for several weeks.

The next six days are sheer hell, as we battle our way through one jungle barricade after another. This is without question the single most strenuous period of physical labor of my life. It is obvious that I have developed a new set of muscles from the herculean effort of "pruning the landscape." By now, the stream has become a clear, dark green color, with a sluggish three-mile-per-hour current, and a meandering course, corkscrewing so radically at times that we found ourselves heading back the way we have come. The channel is still frequently so choked with sizable trees, tenacious vines and dense shrubbery that I have to sharpen my machete every day to cut through the unending jungle.

My machete is useless when we come upon a major log-jam created by two trees, heavy with thick limbs, that had toppled onto each other from opposite banks. This forces us into the drudgery of our first portage. We unload our heaviest baggage, then half carry, half drag the boats around to clear water. The next morning, we bypass a long blockade of overgrowth by towing the kayaks while we wade barefooted through a spongy marsh in water only two feet deep.

As we reach dry ground again, Jack behind me says, "Good Lord! Look at your legs, John!"

After checking mine, I reply, "And look at yours, too, Jack."

We shuddered in disgust at the sight of several slimy

black vampires that have attached themselves to our bare legs. We carefully dislodge and quickly dispatch the little horrors, commonly called leeches, and return to the river.

Just after we push off, I am surprised by the sight of our first crocodile, a six-footer, resting on a mud bar. As I float closer to him he melts into the water and glides rapidly towards me. When the croc has approached to within a few feet, I get on my knees in the cockpit, then raise up and conk him on the head with the flat side of my aluminum paddle, using just enough force to convince him to seek a meal elsewhere. I'm sure he gets the message, since he ducks under and is not seen again.

After a week of bush-busting, the Lualaba has grown into a proper river, with a channel of mostly open water that enables us to paddle freely and unimpeded. This gives us the first good chance to observe and enjoy the diverse wildlife in the area, particularly the birds that constantly flit through the trees, swoop close to us, or swim in the river and soar high overhead. There are spectacular crowned cranes, regal fish eagles (cousin to the American bald eagle), agile black kites, Egyptian geese and sacred ibis, the beautiful lilac-breasted roller, and even wild canaries. Up on the banks, we catch glimpses of waterbuck, blue duikers (a species of small antelope), tree squirrels and Savanna hares (rabbits). One monkey stares at us from a tree, entranced for a few seconds as if he can't believe his eyes. Monitor lizards are a common sight; one is more than four feet long. They are a distant cousin of the Komodo dragon, the largest of all lizards, growing up to ten feet in length and weighing as much as three hundred pounds.

On the seventh day of our strenuous adventure, approximately sixty river miles from the put-in point, we come upon our first waterfall, where the Lualaba noisily surges in a series of frothy cascades over a fifty-foot-wide, ten-foot-high reef of black rock. It is creepy wading in the cold water up to our chests with crocodiles around, but it is the only way we can work the kayaks up to the brink of one of the milder torrents, from where we lower them by rope to the deep pool below and continue.

As I film the falls from below, Jack says, "Do you realize John, that we are likely the first humans to see this waterfall?"

"How's that?" I ask.

"Look at the banks, upstream or down, the river is completely screened all the way along by the thick bush. Standing on either side you can hear the falling water, but the only way you can see the falls is to be right down here in the river."

"I think you're right," I reply. "So far I haven't seen any evidence that anyone, African or white, has ever been on any part of the river, which isn't at all surprising considering how basically impossible it is."

Our eighth day is the most action-packed and interesting one to date. Along the banks we marvel at the sight of what looks like hobgoblin castles, enormous gray termite nests, some of them towering twenty to twenty-five feet tall. Each termitarium represents fifty or more years of masticating, digesting and excreting many tons of earth, the work of countless generations of the white termites.

We come close to two hippos in the river, the first ones we have seen, but they are too drowsy to do anything more than to express a few indignant snorts as we paddle past them. It is a pleasure watching four sable antelope grazing above the water. One of them, a magnificent male, has an astonishing pair of scimitar-shaped horns, at least four feet in length, that sweep upwards over his neck.

The most important of the "firsts" we have been experiencing each day, however, is our first confrontation with rapids. The week of practice in guiding and controlling his kayak has been ideal training in preparing Jack for white-water running. But because the rapids have never been negotiated before, we have to face each one without any information that could be helpful in getting past them.

We sweep through ten rapids during the day. None of them overly violent, but four had tricky, twisting channels, choked with jumbled masses of rock, that tested our ability to zigzag down them without a crack-up.

Jack enters the last swift chute off-center, hangs up on a boulder and swamps. I tow him to shore and, while he towels off and gets into dry clothes, empty the load of water from his kayak.

Our supper this night consists of soup and cheese, even though we are hungry enough to eat a banquet. Our food supplies are getting so low we have begun rationing our meals. No one had warned us about the river thickets that have slowed our progress so drastically, so we had brought provisions sufficient enough for only eight or ten days. Even after eating, our stomachs grumble from hunger.

We have to settle for eight dry prunes each for breakfast, then push off for another day of unexpected escapades. The river fluctuates constantly in width, tapering down in places to only forty feet, then expanding to one hundred farther along. As we paddle through one of the narrows, I hear a gasp from Jack, glance back and am aghast to see him in his kayak perched on the back of a mostly submerged hippo! I quickly backpaddle and move over for a closer look.

Jack, with an expression of absolute terror, is clutching the high side of his boat with both hands, sitting off balance, and appearing as if he is about to fall overboard. "Hang in there, Jack," I whisper, "try not to move. Let's see what he's going to do next." We are well aware of how deadly and unpredictable hippos can be, and that Jack was in serious danger of being capsized and attacked by the huge beast. When the hippo gently and mysteriously lowers Jack and his boat back into the water and vanishes, we are overcome with relief. We paddle rapidly downstream and, when a safe distance away, pull in to rest at a shady inlet. Jack calms down, wiping the nervous sweat from his face, and says, "I feel five years older from this experience." Trying to ease his tension, I say, "Well, in all my clashes with hippos on the Nile, *I* never had the thrill of one playing piggyback with me. I'm kinda jealous!"

The trio of hippos we pass later give us no trouble,

we just "pour on the coals" and whizz past them in such a burst of speed they have no time to react. It would be interesting to know what they were thinking as they watched us shoot by. They'd never before seen anything like us!

During the afternoon, we have four more harrowing rapids to negotiate. The first one is the worst, short but rough, with no visible channels to follow and filled with boulders and turbulence. With no way to portage around, I take a chance and head down in midstream and, after much bouncing around and shipping a lot of water, make it through. I have Jack hike along the bank to the river below, then paddle his kayak to the bottom successfully.

Below the rapids, the Lualaba swells out to two-hundred feet, framed by the foliage that has become more characteristic of the tropics. There were clusters of graceful, lush green palm trees, forests of bamboo and thick-branched

Struggling through ten-foot-tall elephant grass to reach a campsite along the Lualaba (Congo River).

trees soaring to 125 feet. One giant tree is ablaze with large, bright pink flowers that exuded a heady fragrance. We dodge around a *liana*, a jungle vine, thick as a man's waist, that, from a distance, looks like a monstrous python. It hangs down fifty feet from a branch above and nearly touches the water.

When it comes time to reach high ground and camp, we have an excruciatingly difficult struggle penetrating a ten-foot-tall hedge of elephant grass. My machete is now useless against the unyielding wall. We can only force a passage through by pushing, kicking and stomping forward a few feet at a time, the sharp edges of the long blades slashing our arms and legs with small cuts that ooze blood. Adding to our discomfort are concealed clumps of thornbush, which stab us with their needle-sharp spines when we brush against them, and stinging nettle that leaves an itchy rash on our legs.

When we emerge from the grass, our hands, arms and legs look like raw ground beef, but a coating of an antibiotic ointment keeps the gashes from becoming infected and soothes the nettle rashes. For supper we eat, very slowly, a small serving of rice cooked with raisins. Jack performs an enjoyable concert on his harmonica which helps take our minds off our hunger.

I wake up stiff and sore, feeling as though my back will never again be normal, bruised by the rigorous exertion of bushwhacking, paddling and sleeping on the hard ground. Another spartan meal of oatmeal and dried fruit. *Oh!* I thought, *for a decent breakfast of orange juice, pancakes, eggs, toast and hash browns!*

We haven't been on the river fifteen minutes when we come upon a steep, rock-bound chute of white water, the only route we can take to continue down-river, because of the lack of navigable channels, but a route which proves my undoing.

Jack, knowing this would make a good action sequence for the documentary record of our expedition, lands and tramps through the brambles along the shore until he can station himself at the base of the rapid. When he is in position, he calls out for me to start the run and begins filming with the 16mm movie camera.

I push off the islet where I'd been waiting, paddle forward until the kayak is captured by the racing current, and swoop down the narrow corridor at a giddy speed. It is a wild ride, yet I make it through without hitting any rocks. My luck runs out though just at the end of the rapid, when my momentum causes me to crash into a half-submerged boulder in the middle of the flood and directly in front of Jack and the camera. It results in an absorbing, but costly, sequence for the film. The surging torrent engulfs the damaged boat, causing it to sink, overturn and break in two at the center. I scramble out and use all my strength clinging to the heavy, water-filled shell, keeping it from being washed away by the swift current. With a series of strong tugs and pulls, I am able to wrestle the kayak to dry land and survey the damage.

It is disheartening to find even more crippling damage than I suspected. The kayak is an appalling wreck, the collision with the boulder had fractured the center brace bar and the framework's backbone, as well as two top spars on either side. The terrific strain imposed by the heavy current has splintered the cross-support in the stern. This minor disaster brings to a head the resentment I have been feeling from the beginning about the totally inaccurate information about the Lualaba, provided by authorities who should have known better or should have admitted not having knowledge about the upper river. One of the men confidently informed us that the river began by flowing out of a marsh. "Look out for the crocodiles there," he advised us. Other officials told us that once we found enough water to float the kayaks, "Don't worry, you can just put your boats in the river and paddle off, there are no rapids for two hundred miles."

These same individuals also let us know that it wasn't necessary for us to take too large a supply of food for our trip because we could stop at villages along the river and buy chickens, eggs, fish, sweet potatoes and beans from the villagers.

Originally, we had thought this advice was invaluable in giving us an impression of what to expect on the river, but now, from our personal experience, we had found it to be entirely wrong.

The source, for example, is definitely not a marsh, but a spring; below the source, the Lualaba is so choked with trees and brush growing out of the water it was almost unnavigable for at least sixty miles. Even beyond that, there are still occasional thickets in the river that impede our progress. Moreover, in ten days of travel we didn't see one village on either bank, so there was no way to supplement our limited food supplies. Finally, the unexpected series of rapids, some of them, such as this last one, were life-threatening, and, without a doubt, many more to contend with ahead.

Even our detailed maps were useless since they showed no indication of rapids until far downstream.

We had the battered kayak reassembled by noontime, replacing the vital brace bar with a spare from our emergency kit and splicing the other broken pieces with twine and nylon fishing line. It takes us half a day to portage both boats three hundred yards through the dense undergrowth and slashing grass of the eastern shore to a flat, dry hippo landing, below the last white water.

We make three sweltering additional trips to transport our equipment to the landing, lugging the heavy bags on our backs and then loading them in the kayaks again. We are so worn out by the overland portages there is a temptation to make camp right on the hippo landing, but we are worried about being trampled during the night by the nocturnally foraging animals. (Each year a number of Africans, sleeping on the banks of lakes or rivers, are killed by hippos stepping on them in the dark.)

As dusk approaches we run a short but vigorous rapid and, just below, reach a waterfall that requires some serious scouting and can't be tackled in the fading light. We fetch up on a small island for the night and are lulled to sleep by the roar of the falls, but not before treating ourselves to our last can of delicious minestrone soup, heated over a bamboo fire.

"Isn't it strange," asks Jack, "that during the day I'm too busy to be really conscious of how hungry I am, but when we eat, I realize how starved I feel?"

"That's right," I reply, "it's the same with me. None of our snacks we call meals satisfy me. I'm always much more hungry after eating. We've both lost a lot of weight."

The next five days are dominated by a nightmare of rapids, two dozen uncharted, untraveled, life-endangering stretches that range from waterfalls to thunderous cataracts. This is an emotionally trouble-some time for Jack and me. Since there is no alternative but to pass over them, we have to discipline ourselves as never before, repress our fears and remain in steady control of our feelings in order to execute the intricate moves and make the quick decisions necessary to choose the safest channels. My kayak is sluggish and unstable from the damaged framework and presented me with a real problem when guiding it in the rapids. It handled with all the agility of a tugboat.

I am filled with admiration for Jack, in the way he always faces our difficulties and dangers, particularly the deadly rapids, with courage and a witty sense of humor. He demonstrates genuine bravery in mastering the anxiety and dread he feels whenever we paddle through white-water areas.

From having lived in Africa all his life my partner knows how dangerous hippos, crocodiles and rapids can be, yet he endures each of them unflinchingly. We have grown as close as brothers during the journey, bonded by the incredible experiences and hardships we have been sharing. One such hazardous event occurs as we laze along down a quiet area heavy with fragrance one morning, paddling side by side through one of the loveliest landscapes we have seen, with luxuriant emerald green jungle on both banks, enhanced by gorgeous sprays of orchids and other beautiful flowering plants. Our peaceful mood is rudely shattered as we round a bank and surprise a lone hippo in the river. He immediately protests our intrusion into his territory by plunging toward us in a fast charge that forces us to paddle for our lives. I am astonished at how fast the three-ton monster moved, but accelerated by fright, we are able to go faster and escape.

Later, as I pass a high, brushy bank, a nine-foot crocodile shoots out of the undergrowth above me, dives into the river and squeezes underneath my kayak to deep water, leaving me with a dry-as-cotton mouth and wildly speeded up heartbeat.

There are only a few times when I am able to make a survey of a rapid to scout out the best channels. A rapid inspection is a grueling chore, which involves struggling along the shore as close to the river as possible, wading through shadowy pools of water up to my waist with strange things brushing against my legs under a thick canopy of vines and snake-like lianas; battling through thick stands of bamboo and a riot of tropical plants; stirring up clouds of mosquitoes and other biting insects; and slogging through muddy hippo wallows, spattered with fresh tracks.

On one such excursion I fell into an abandoned burrow of the world's fastest mammal excavator, the aardvark, and became the world's fastest moving human, as I scrambled out of the pit to escape a possible cobra or other venomous snake known for their habit of making such a tunnel their den. Just the day before I had spotted a five-foot boomslang, a green snake that has a toxic venom more lethal than a cobra's or mamba's.

When I was able to scan some of the shorter rapids on foot, I found a mental rehearsal helpful in planning the course we should follow, practicing the run several times by visualizing it clearly in my mind. I had developed this technique during the passage through one of the difficult cataracts of the Nile River and ever since have found it invaluable for a variety of uses, from lecturing before an audience of thousands to the sports of skydiving and scuba diving.

It is not possible to make a survey on foot when we arrive in our kayaks at the longest and most difficult expanse of rough water we have seen on the Lualaba. This cataract is a mile long, its course complicated by a labyrinth of channels sweeping through a number of rocky islands, overgrown with greenery. We have to twist, dodge, backpaddle and dart forward to avoid the rocks in the rushing water, but we come through without crashing or capsizing.

During the morning of our sixteenth day since leaving the village of Kikuyu, we race through six rapids in succession, with adrenaline-charged excitement in each one. But this is nothing like the elation we feel when, after the dash through the last rapid, we behold an amazing surprise—a motor launch heading upstream towards us bearing three white men, the first whites we have seen in seventeen days and in two hundred miles of travel on the Lualaba.

The men include the territorial administrator and his two friends, both geologists, from the copper mines at Kolwezi, thirty-five miles from the river. Because we are a week overdue from our expected arrival at Kolwezi, the provincial governor, had personally asked the territorial administrator to conduct a search mission, to try to find us. The appearance of our searchers couldn't have been better timed, because the launch, moving upriver, would have soon been stopped by the rapids. If we hadn't met the men below the rapids, they would have had to return empty-handed to Kolwezi. We would had two more long days of additional travel "on empty" because we have used up all our food, with the exception of a large fish I had caught.

With the kayaks in tow, Jack and I climb aboard the launch, and for the first time since leaving the put-in, enjoy an effortless ride over the water. The territorial administrator says to us, "If we hadn't found you today a government plane was going to continue the search tomorrow from the air. The governor wants a full report on your experiences. He knows you are the first to travel down the river from its beginning, and he's anxious to record details on what you've seen for his official records."

We spent a week in Kolwezi, enjoying the advantages of civilization again, especially the ample food, warm hospitality and comfortable beds. I located a carpenter who was able to build new parts to replace the broken ones on my kayak. Then, after buying fresh provisions, it is time to return to the river.

On the last day before reaching Bukama, Jack and I are full of high spirits as we arise on a brilliant July morning in the bamboo grove

Fonda Biabo, first village on Congo River, three hundred miles downstream, with me climbing its twenty-five-foot termite nest. This termitarium is possibly the largest in Africa.

where we have spent the cold night. We are excited at the prospect of reaching one of our major goals, the little port of Bukama, just a few hours downstream. By arriving at Bukama we become the first to have successfully explored the first 375 miles of the Lualaba, the least known and one of the most difficult stretches of the mighty Congo River. We dispense with breakfast, hurriedly load the kayaks and push off. We cautiously thread our way down one of several rapids-ridden channels, filtering through a maze of lushly overgrown islands, and soon arrive where the divided river converges again into one main channel, bounded by boulder-strewn banks.

The banks rise steeply around us as we glide along, until we find ourselves in a narrow gorge, sweeping forward at a rapid clip in the grip of a powerful current. Just five miles upstream the Lualaba had been an impressive water course, with a breadth of two hundred yards and more. Here, in the chasm, this massive flow compresses between solid walls of glistening rock averaging only twenty-five yards apart.

With the river straining furiously at her confining corset of granite, we shoot through a succession of rapids. We fight to stay upright and afloat. The water churns and boils under us with malevolent force, tossing our light craft around like chips. Several times we hold our breath as we are drawn downwards into the gurgling maws of great sucking whirlpools, which roil round our kayaks like Satan's imps, causing them to twirl and tilt dangerously. We feel helpless in their grasp. To struggle too vigorously in evading them means certain upset, as the margin of balance is small in our narrow-beamed cockleshells.

As we grapple with the fearsome boils I get the scare of my life as we round a bend and hear the lusty roar of heavy turbulence close by. The clamor from the crashing water fills me with fear for, just the day before, we had been solemnly warned by several African fishermen to be on guard for a giant, impassable waterfall a few miles downstream. From the loudly echoing din ahead I am convinced that we have reached the falls. We cast about wildly, seeking an escape, as the surging river bears us inexorably on at a dizzying rate towards the unseen cataract. With a flurry of powerful strokes we manage to break free of the current and reach the safety of a backwater next to the left bank, where we anchor to a great boulder. Jack sits patiently while I scramble over the rocky landscape to make a reconnaissance of the river and decide what our next move will be. I am relieved to discover that the thunder filling the canyon is being produced not by the unnavigable waterfalls described by the fishermen, but by the river tumbling tumultuously over three rock-studded cascades, with a tricky S-shape twisting to its course. As is our habit of long practice in coming upon hazardous white water, I paddle first Jack's, then my kayak, through, while my partner hikes to the base of the rapids. During the first passage I have a close call and nearly wreck Jack's boat when the violent torrent slams me into a mass of sharp rock with a spine-jarring jolt as I thrash around the second bend. Fortunately, I am able to swing the nose at the last second before the collision so that only two cross braces are fractured instead of the vital baseboard or some other irreplaceable part. For a hectic minute I teeter precariously on the rocky perch as the current tears savagely at me; then I finally wedge my paddle firmly in a crevice, wrench myself off and debouch unharmed. There are tense moments in getting my own boat down the formidable chutes, but I make it safely. We bail out the gallons of water that have filled the two boats during the rough white-water run. Then I repair the damaged kayak by nailing flattened tin sardine cans over the breaks in the crossbars. Within an hour after encountering this hindrance to our progress, we are underway again, Jack paddling in my undamaged kayak for safety's sake and I in his.

At midday we arrive at the head of a narrow and steeply dropping defile, down which the Lualaba swoops with terrific force. This we recognize unmistakably as the waterfall described by the fishermen. We tie up in a little cove and proceed to examine this wonder and figure a way to bypass it. As we stand transfixed by the awesome sight at our feet we hear, above the tumult, a hearty shout of *"Jambo sana!"* the traditional Swahili greeting, and turn to see a grinning African approaching. We delight at seeing a human in this remote territory, but the man is astonished at seeing us. We happily shake his hand as he explains that he had been fishing near his camp below the falls when he spotted us standing on the rocks.

We spend the next hour in leisurely fashion, filming the impressive cataract (which we named Grosvenor Falls in honor of the illustrious family that founded the National Geographic Society), collecting unusual specimens to add to my growing entomological collection, bringing our journals up to date and taking lessons from our newfound friend on how to fish with a dip net.

The friendly fisherman tells us he had visited a Catholic mission as a boy and had been given the name of Joseph by the priest. Joseph shows us his camp, where his lame brother is busily smoking the morning catch of barbel and minnows. I examine his leg and find it swollen from a thorn infection. Breaking out our well-equipped medical kit, I give the grateful African a generous supply of sulfa pills with instructions on how and when to take them, which Jack translates into fluent Swahili. This little gesture really cements our friendship.

The day is wearing on by now, and as we are enjoying the unprecedented respite so greatly, I suggest to Jack that we utilize the remainder of the daylight hours in filming the general details of our daily life that we had been planning to record for so long.

"I know the men would be pleased to have us spend the night with them, and then we can get an early start for Bukama in the morning," I say.

"That sounds well and good to me, John," he replies, "but on the other hand this cold of mine does seem to be getting worse, and I could really use a good night's sleep in a real bed. Why don't we pick up and carry on now?"

The thought of resting in a comfortable bed instead of on the cold hard ground, and of appetizing food, seems irresistible to me, too. "What are we waiting for?" I respond enthusiastically.

With our plans settled we bid *"Kwaheri"* to our friends, hop into our boats and paddle vigorously upstream, hugging the left bank just out of the pull of the strong current. Reaching a respectable distance above the falls we put on a burst of speed and dash across the river to the opposite side. There is no way to bypass the big chute on the left except by a long and arduous portage overland, so we now take advantage of a small side channel branching off just to the right of the falls and entering the river again a hundred yards downstream. It would have been foolhardy to paddle down to this detour. The river is much too swift and there is too great a risk of being hurled right into the falls before making the turn into the side channel. We climb out to ease the boats down by means of their anchor ropes, but Jack slips and falls heavily on the rocks, bruising his legs. I sit him in the shade of a tree to recuperate while I continue the operation.

I work his kayak along the bank and then down the passage as far as possible. I return for my boat and push off as my companion, now recovered, trudges downstream. Just as I reach the entrance to the detour, directly above the falls, I step out on a half-submerged boulder to maneuver the skittish craft around. The rock topples over, throwing me off balance, and I find myself in the churning water. I lose hold of the rope as the kayak veers sideways, and I am drawn by the surge towards the thundering maelstrom.

Floundering to the shell I grab the prow, turn it facing down the chute and give it a hefty shove forward with all my strength. Then, realizing my dangerous position, I swim rapidly back to shore. With huge relief I climb out and see that my timely push had been just enough to line up the kayak on a straight course and send it coasting down the falls without capsizing. I race to keep it from being carried off downstream. Diving in again, I stroke over, climb into the cockpit and paddle down to land near the beached kayak.

Jack and I first unload the equipment bags of the first kayak, lugging them a hundred feet from the side channel to the river's edge. After a brief rest we sweatily portage the boat. The rocks are slick and treacherous underfoot as we stagger over them. Again Jack loses his footing and falls, gashing his knees painfully. While he relaxes and nurses his wounds I trek downstream for more than a half mile to study the river and confirm the information Joseph had given me. The African had told us there are no more rough places like the falls, and that the few rapids remaining shouldn't be too much trouble as they are not as bad as some of those upstream.

In looking over the white water I find this to be accurate. The rapids here are relatively mild compared to many we have run successfully. I am sure Jack will have no difficulty with them. During the past month he has developed real skill and proficiency in handling his kayak. By now he has been through nearly four times the number of rapids that I had run when we first started the expedition. He seems to keenly enjoy the excitement of white water and goes swooping along with "yahoos" of pure delight.

Even so, I don't feel we should take any chances, now that we are so near Bukama. As I return to him, I consider suggesting that he hike around the rapids overland and let me handle the kayaks on the river. I change my mind, though, upon seeing how his bruises make him limp and gasp with pain. As a precautionary measure I float my boat around a rocky reef jutting into the water so he can be lined up directly for the first rapid. I get him loaded and settled in the cockpit, with the spray covers firmly in place. I hurry to the other kayak, get myself ready, then launch out into the river.

The little boat, thrown out of alignment by the morning accident, handles sluggishly. I have a terrible time controlling it. As I struggle to head in the right direction, the current sweeps me against a big tower of rock at the head of the cascade. Here I am stuck fast until I can swing around and begin moving again. Jack, endeavoring to stick close, shoots ahead and is forced to go on as I hang up. Jack takes the lead for the first time of the expedition.

Seconds later I gain control of my balky craft and start down the swift chute. At the foot of the rapid I see Jack facing upstream in slack water. Seeing I am in no difficulty and proceeding close behind, he noses about and glides out of sight, to the right of another big monolith of stone, although I have cautioned him to go down the left side because of more intense turbulence on the right. I am not too worried, for I know the water around the rock is not excessively rough. It is a genuine shock then, in passing the outcropping, to behold Jack's kayak, fifty yards beyond, drifting gently in a backwater upside down, and my friend nowhere to be seen. For a moment I can't believe my eyes. It doesn't seem possible that Jack could have capsized in merely passing down the short gush of agitated water swirling around the monolith.

With a chilling sense of anxiety I quickly scan the sides of the river, trying to see whether he has reached land safely. Then I glance downstream and catch sight of him bobbing along in mid-channel near the end of the next rapid. Shouting after him with all my lung power, "Hang on, Jack! I'm coming!" I flail forward as fast as I can paddle in a frantic effort to rescue my stricken companion. My unbalanced boat veers back and forth like a pendulum as I breast the turbulence of the rampaging water. I shoot through and somehow emerge upright, but have little time to look again before I am engulfed in the turmoil of the fourth and final cascade of the series.

In my urgent haste I rocket over the surface at reckless speed—much too fast a pace for an unstable little kayak. In the midst of the rapid it swerves into high choppy waves and flips over on top of me.

It is impossible to remain on the surface, where at least I can breathe. I am helpless in the powerful grip of erratic boils, which suck me down so deep my ears ache from the pressure, then shoot me upwards in a violent hydraulic action. I churn around this way and that, totally out of control, and as dizzy as if I am trapped in a giant cement mixer. The savage crosscurrents force my arms and legs to flail around with such force that it seems they will be pulled from their sockets. Only during a lull in the turbulence am I able to capture my limbs by rolling myself into a ball, with my head bent down between my knees, and my arms encircling and locking around my lower legs. My struggles to return to the surface are useless; they only burn up energy that needs to be conserved to enable me to hold my breath as long as possible. I realize my only chance of surviving is to relax and hold out long enough for the river to carry me to quiet water. I will myself to calm down and control my fear.

As I near the final seconds of my endurance, a surge

rams water up my nose, forcing me to cough underwater. I swallow a big gulp before I can close my mouth. I have to let go of my pent-up air with a loud whoosh just as I break the surface, sucking in a breath that is as much water as air. As the current carries me out of the turbulence I quickly revive, growing stronger with every breath.

Upon recovering my kayak I hoist myself atop the wet hull and begin scanning the water and banks intently for some sign of my partner Jack, calling out his name as I float downstream on the now-subdued river.

Finding nothing, I recover my paddle, work the water-logged shell to a landing on the eastern shore and then dash along the banks shouting for my missing friend. I clamber to the top of a high ledge where I have a commanding view of the river. As I stand there, anxiously surveying the riverscape, I feel a shudder of horror as Jack's overturned kayak comes drifting silently by—like a ghostly phantom—followed closely by his pipe, and then a box of matches, bobbing along on the surface.

Though there is no other evidence of Jack, my mind refuses to accept that he might have drowned. He is a strong swimmer and I picture him lying safe, but unseen, somewhere on either shore, too exhausted to answer my calls. I know that if he has landed anywhere behind me he will eventually return to the fisherman's camp.

But in the more likely possibility that he has been carried further downstream, I return to my beached kayak to prepare it for continuing the search. My state of frenzy gives me such a rush of adrenaline that I am able to grab the prow of my swamped boat, lift it to chest level, tip it and drain it, even though with its load of water and baggage it must weigh more than two hundred pounds. I fling out all of the cumbersome equipment bags and, taking only my powerful binoculars, launch forth into the river.

With sinking hope I drift downstream, searching and calling out fruitlessly. There are no more rapids, only a few minor riffles, then finally a calm, ever-broadening river. Upon catching up with Jack's runaway kayak, I pause to turn it upright, empty the water, then take it in tow. Farther along I salvage the floating paddle.

Joseph had said Bukama was *"Karibu sana!"*—very close—so I decide to continue and organize a search party at the small settlement. The capsizing had occurred about 3:30, but not until 6:00 in the evening do I finally sight the first of the two steel bridges near the town. The river expands rapidly in width as I glide over its placid surface, and as I round the bend down from the bridge, it expands to two hundred yards. In the distance I see the small port with a paddlewheel steamer tied up dockside. Here is the Congo River's head of navigation.

Africans in slender dugouts hail me in passing, but I am too distressed to answer. I methodically thrash at the water until I spot two figures in the twilight, landing a small launch on the right bank near the second bridge. Remarkably one of them turns out to be the gentleman I most want to see, Monsieur Emile Parent, the territorial administrator. The other man is Phillip Osley, a young professional fisherman.

As I briefly describe the calamitous accident, Monsieur Parent immediately springs into action. While Osley drives me to the local rest house and procures for me a change of clothing, the territorial administrator alerts his assistant and some askaris. At 7:00 P.M. I jump into a pickup truck with six askaris and Oliver Dupres, the young assistant administrator, and drive with them to a local village near the first bridge. Here we recruit fourteen more Africans to participate in the search for Jack. By 8 P.M. twenty-two of us are quick marching through thick bush over a narrow, rocky trail that leads, by a circuitous route, to a small abandoned fishing village near the big waterfall. My heart fills with a fervent prayer that Jack has somehow hauled himself out of the water and made it back to Joseph's camp for the night.

It takes two hours of fast trekking to reach the cluster of old grass huts. Here we hold up for a time, casting about with our lanterns and flashlights before finding the faint path that leads down through the thick undergrowth to the river.

Upon glimpsing Joseph's fire, I sprint ahead and burst upon the sleeping camp, desperately hoping to see that Jack is with them. I find only the two startled Africans. Our urgent questions only draw blank looks from them. They have seen nothing, know nothing. When they are filled in about the missing bwana, they insist on joining us as we move on along the river's edge.

We scrutinize the banks to a point well below the rapids where I had last seen my companion, but we are disappointed; there is nothing to see with our flashlights but the swift, churning water studded with black rocks. Leaving all but three of the men for the few remaining hours of the night to continue the search at dawn, Dupres and I trudge wearily back to Bukama where we sadly report our lack of success. I feel physically sick from shock and grief, and I can't sleep, despite my exhaustion from the long day and the fourteen-mile search mission.

During the next four days the search effort is carried on by an augmented ground party of fifty men who comb the banks from the falls to the bridge. Two reconnaissance planes from the Kamina Air Base, 110 miles from Bukama, orbit the river repeatedly. Twice, five of us travel upstream in a government launch, anxiously scanning the banks and river for any sign of Jack. Upon reaching white water, we land and then tramp along the rugged banks until we reach the scene of the capsizing, where we stand like statues, staring in silence at the mesmerizing rapids. Still, we find nothing. My luckless partner has completely vanished. We all share an unspoken fear that he has been taken by crocodiles.

At last, on the morning of the fifth day, as we are about to abandon hope of ever finding him, Jack's floating body is discovered by one of the local villagers, wedged between two dugouts near the Bukama dock. As there are no bruises on him, it seems that Jack must have drowned in the powerful whirlpools infesting the rapids area. Thus has my friend and colleague, Jack Yowell, perished at the untimely age of thirty-six. His tragic death abruptly terminates one of the closest and warmest friendships I have known. We had shared some of the most incredible adventures and intense hardships of our lives. Always he endured each one with gallant bravery and an impish sense of humor.

We are able to summon an English minister, Reverend Harold Berry, from a nearby village to conduct a funeral service in the afternoon. The ceremony is attended by the ten white citizens of Bukama and several of the askaris who had helped in the search mission. It seems bitterly ironic that Jack should lose his life in the very last stretch of white water before reaching Bukama and a peaceful, wide-open river—especially considering that we had successfully negotiated 125 unknown and unexplored rapids from the source, many of them even more violent.

In reflecting on his passing I recall one of Jack's favorite sayings, which he applied to every major event of his full life: "Sometimes only God knows it, but there's a good reason for everything that happens to us!" In the spirit of this philosophy, Winifred Yowell accepted the death of her husband with a feeling of deep pride from his having made an important contribution to African geography by making the first-ever exploration of the wild upper course of the world's second largest river.

On the first day of our expedition, Jack and I made a promise to each other that, in a crisis, if one of us was lost, the survivor would then carry on alone to complete the project. After the funeral, and during the next three months, I continued downstream from Bukama, tracing the great watercourse all the way to the Atlantic—for both of us.

LIFE GOAL #4: *Explore the Colorado River*

Close Encounter with the Colorado River

xploration is the field I most wanted to follow as a lifetime career. At an early age I read biographies of great explorers. Through reading their journals, several of these men became personal heroes and role models to me. Men like Marco Polo, Sir Francis Drake, Captain James Cook, Lewis and Clark, and those paragons of African exploration, Henry Morton Stanley and Dr. Livingston, are just a few of my all-time favorites. And what extraordinary exemplars they are for anyone! Each of these individuals was a powerful man of destiny, who dared to penetrate into the unknown, resolutely facing every kind of danger, from warlike cultures to aggressive wildlife, debilitating diseases and violent extremes of weather.

Of the nineteenth century American explorers, other than Lewis and Clark, one explorer stands out: Major John Wesley Powell, a former Union officer who lost his right arm to a Confederate sharpshooter during the Battle of Shiloh. After the war, Powell became a first-rate surveyor, geologist and ethnologist. Of all his many achievements, one in particular aroused my greatest interest and deepest admiration.

In 1869, despite having only one arm, Major Powell led a team of nine men, traveling in four wooden boats, on a one-thousand-mile expedition down the unmapped Colorado and Green rivers. During the trip, they passed through areas no one—not even Indians—had ever seen! Powell's dramatic descriptions of exploring the uncharted Grand Canyon, where he and his companions ran one violent cataract after another with no idea of what lay ahead, makes enthralling reading for anyone to this day.

Reading about Major Powell's river adventures stimulated dreams of experiencing my own trip through "the Great Unknown," as he called the Grand Canyon. Though this ambition was never abandoned, other goals took precedence for me: military service as a flier in the Fifteenth Air Force, serving a mission for my church in Canada and Minnesota, graduating from USC, serving a tour of duty in the Merchant Marine, and a filming expedition through Mexico and Central America. My number-one goal: carrying out the first successful exploration of the 4,200-mile Nile River, a ten-month-long project in itself.

Finally, the time and finances become available to make the Grand Canyon dream come true. By then, the goal has expanded dramatically, including producing a documentary film about the Colorado River, and journeying from its Rocky Mountain source in Colorado to where it finishes 1,440 miles downstream in Mexico. I plan to travel by rubber paddle raft, outboard motorboat and cabin cruiser on various stretches of the river and its huge reservoirs. To enhance the quality of the film, I want to combine aerial scenes with ground footage to provide a bird's-eye view of the river and the surrounding terrain.

The problem of arranging for an aircraft for the aerial photography is quickly solved during one of my annual lecture tours. En route to Boise, Idaho, I stop off in Twin Falls to visit my friend Walt Blaylock, a likable, softspoken, easygoing man—a professional photographer with whom I share many interests, including our lifelong love of adventure and flying.

When I describe my plan to Walt, he immediately becomes enthusiastic about the adventure and suggests he fly us in his private plane and also accompany me on the Canyon trip. This is good news indeed!

After the lecture tour, I return home, eager to arrange details of the project, making reservations for a three-week raft trip through the Grand Canyon beginning in June. By the middle of May, I return to Twin Falls, ready to begin the aerial filming portion of the project. The day after my arrival, Walt and I get an early start at the local airport. We load equipment aboard his single-engine aluminum Cessna. We take off, tanks full of fuel and heads full of plans, on a picture perfect, cloudless morning, setting a compass heading for Lake Granby, a distance of 480 miles from Twin Falls. This is the Colorado River's source, at the head of one of its two branches, in north central Colorado.

With excellent weather conditions and detailed maps, we enjoy contact flying—maintaining an accurate course by visually identifying ground features as they appear. By noon, despite minor head winds, we come within sight of Granby, an eight-mile-long, club-shaped lake created by snowmelt and drainage from the surrounding mountains of the beautiful Rocky Mountain National Park. As our plane descends, heading toward the western side of the lake, I begin filming with my sixteen-millimeter camera. As we drop closer to the water, a wonderful sight appears—a rare marvel of geography that for many years existed only in my imagination. Emerging from the lake in its first existence, appearing as a gentle trout stream and gleaming in the bright sunshine—the actual birth of one of America's most vital rivers—the mighty Colorado! This is an emotional moment for me—the beginning of fulfilling my boyhood dream of traveling the length of the Colorado River.

When our fuel is nearly exhausted, we fly to nearby Granby Airfield, make a bouncy landing on the earthen runway and taxi over to a fuel site where the attendant tops off the wing tanks. After stretching our legs, we eat tuna sandwiches, always a favorite of mine on these excursions, then climb back into the plane to continue the flight over the river downstream. Walt taxis down the length of the runway, swings the plane around and prepares for takeoff.

After a final instrument and controls check, he slowly advances the throttle to full power to test the engine, releases the brakes and moves forward. We are both anxious about the thin air density since temperature and altitude directly affect the performance of an aircraft. The air temperature hovers around seventy degrees and Granby Airport lies at a lofty altitude of over eight thousand feet above sea level—the highest elevation from which either of us has ever flown a plane. These two factors increase the takeoff distance by over 250 percent and decrease our rate of climb by 75 percent, as compared to takeoff and climbing from an airport at sea level at sixty degrees!

Walt begins the takeoff as close to the beginning of the airstrip as possible to allow for a long run and safe liftoff. The plane bounces along interminably over the rough, unpaved surface, distressingly sluggish and slow in gaining speed. With the end of the runway looming up alarmingly close, Walt pulls back the yoke and the Cessna lurches into the air. Even with full power, the insurmountable combination of a takeoff at such a high altitude and the heavy load of fresh fuel cause the plane to struggle to achieve a gradual climb. We manage to reach an altitude of four hundred feet when a sudden violent wind rushes head-on over our faltering plane, buffeting us with such turbulence that we lose critical flying speed. As drag increases, our lift is suddenly reduced to zero. A sickening sense of doom creeps over me as the controls become mushy and unresponsive. We are startled by the sudden jarring sound of a warning horn going off, as we experience one of the most dangerous and frightening calamities that can happen in flying—a stall-out!

Walt switches off the engine since its power is inadequate to control the Cessna in the blustery gusts. It's an eerie sensation to be high in the air, aboard a propeller-driven vehicle, when the engine grows suddenly silent and the only sounds are the ghostly rumbles and flutters of the wind against the aircraft.

Out of control, we begin falling off in a sharp right bank, the plane about to go into a death spin. Though appearing outwardly calm, Walt's eyes are wide with fear. His hands look bloodless from gripping the yoke so tightly. Desperate thoughts of *What can we do? What can we do?* shoot through my mind. I resist an instinctive urge to grab my yoke and pull it back, knowing there is nothing either of us can do to keep us from plummeting to earth. Nevertheless, I find myself stomping down on the floor with both feet in a futile, almost comical effort to somehow stop our steep fall.

With the nose down, the slight increase of speed enables Walt to gain enough control to level the wings and keep us from sinking into the fatal spin, but even so, the Cessna plunges into an uncontrollable dive. Helpless, we stare spellbound at the treeless green earth rushing toward us. It's like looking at the ground through a zoom lens, with it rapidly growing in size and detail by the second.

"Great God in heaven, we're going to crash, Walt!" I shout.

"Yeah," he replied over the din of the rushing air. "It's going to be bad, John. Brace yourself."

I hitch my seat belt as tightly as possible, straighten my legs and prop my feet firmly on the floor below the rudder pedals. Whenever I am on the verge of dying, my first impulse is to express a silent prayer to the Almighty for deliverance. I have just uttered such a petition when the plane smashes into the ground with stunning force and a loud *whomp* that sounds like a muffled explosion. An instant after hitting the surface, the Cessna flips over on its back.

Barely conscious, dazed by shock and pain, we hang upside-down, immobilized by the crack-up. Finally, awareness returns with the opening of my eyes. My body hurts in a dozen places. Blood rushing to my head causes my brain to whirl with vertigo until I am nauseous. My legs are numb from the tight lap belt. At first I see only a bright, formless image, and I fear that the trauma of the crash has impaired my vision. Then, as my head clears, I realize that what I'm seeing, from my topsy-turvy perspective, is our battered windscreen. At the moment of impact, my heavy movie camera had been wrenched from my grasp, flying into the Plexiglas and buckling it on my side of the cabin.

I glance over at my companion. His face is bloody and he's just coming out of his stupor. I manage to gasp, "We're down in one piece, Walt, and we're still alive. It's a real miracle, isn't it?" There's no response. "Are you okay?"

Like a whiff of smelling salts, the acrid odor of leaking fuel rouses me to the danger of fire. I release my belt and fall in a pain-wracked heap to the floor, which is really the roof. My knees feel like they have been decapitated from striking the yoke and instrument panel with such violent force. I release Walt from his confining lap belt and ease him down to an upright position. He has a deep open cut along his left eye that's oozing blood and a smaller laceration on top of his head. We both have numerous bruises, but seemingly no broken bones.

Working as quickly as possible, I push the bent door open with my feet and we crawl outside to survey the damage to the plane. The Cessna is a complete wreck, from the splintered wooden propeller to the battered vertical stabilizer. The impact has left the landing struts and wheels splayed apart to twice their normal width.

"Lucky for us the ground here is soft and swampy," Walt says, just now regaining his wits. "John, if we had hit at a steeper angle on hard ground, or if we had come down in any one of the dense forests hereabouts, we would have been killed for sure."

"That's right," I agree, looking over the wrecked plane. "Or, we would have been cooked if the tanks had ruptured and all of our fuel had exploded. And look how close we came to drowning!" I point to where the plane's left wing rests, partly submerged, in the glistening Colorado.

"Just three or four yards farther and we would have crashed right into the river," Walt reports.

"Kind of shocking, isn't it?"

At the sound of voices, we turn and see four men running toward us from across a grassy field. After shaking hands and introductions, one of the men explains, "We were fishing on the riverbank, about half a mile from here!"

"Yeah, we saw you dive down and hit the ground," says one concerned-looking fisherman.

"Dropped everything to rush over, expecting to recover bodies, but here you are walking around!" exclaims the first man on the scene.

"More like hobbling around," Walt remarks. "But you know the old saying, 'Any landing you can walk away from. . . .'"

The other men agree with nods.

After inspecting the battered Cessna, the men help us turn the plane right side up. When they see the extent of the damage, they are incredulous that we didn't suffer more serious injuries. We convince them that, except for Walt needing a few stitches, we really have survived the accident in remarkably good condition, and all that is needed is a few days of recovery from our general aches and pains. "Well, you boys were either born under very lucky stars or you've got great guardian angels," marvels one of the men.

"It could be one or the other . . . or even both!" I reply.

LIFE GOAL #123: *Travel Through the Grand Canyon on Foot and by Boat*

Devil's Highway— The Demonic Colorado River

O n June 15, Walt and I reunite at Lee's Ferry in the colorful Red Rock Canyon country of northern Arizona. This spot is the put-in for raft trips through the Grand Canyon, located on the banks of a now-robust, silt-brown Colorado River.

Both of us have recovered from the injuries suffered in the plane crash, and we are now eager to get started on what we are sure will be one of the greatest experiences of our lives: the twenty-two-day, 310-mile expedition from Lee's Ferry to Temple Bar Landing on Lake Mead in Nevada.

Our group consists of twelve people, eight men and four women, all of us, with the exception of Walt, from California. Floating in the shallows at riverside are our three rafts—black inflatable boats of neoprene rubber, with eight-foot yellow oars. Walt and I stand looking at them from the base of the sloping dirt launching ramp. I turn to him and ask, "Are you thinking what I'm thinking, Walt? Don't these boats look awfully *dinky?* They're not even as long as my sixteen-foot kayaks I used on the Nile and Congo Rivers in Africa!"

"Right," drawls Walt, "and with four people in each raft, plus all the food, cooking and camping gear and our personal stuff, we're going to have one cozy ride."

Our misgivings increase when we meet and hear from our river guide, Georgie White. She is a deeply tanned, fortyish woman with a weathered face, wearing a red shirt, red shorts and a frizzy yellow straw hat. She assembles everyone in the shade of a tamarisk tree for a briefing on our trip and to discuss safety precautions, emergency procedures and the need for everyone to work together as a team. Everyone sits up attentively as she informs us, "By the time this trip is over, you folks will join a very special class of pioneer river runners. The Park Service informs me that only 189 people have been through the Grand Canyon before us, so we'll break the two hundred mark by the time we reach Lake Mead!"* Our colorful guide also reveals that our trip will be only the second time she's been through the Grand Canyon, the first run having been a training excursion with

---

*This was in 1954.

an experienced guide. With pride in her voice she announces that nine of us are her first clients, and our trip together will make her the first woman to operate a commercial river-running business on the Colorado River.

Though everyone else accepts this startling information with quiet resignation and disperses to collect their gear, Walt and I hang back to discuss our concerns.

"Talk about learning on the job, Walt. I can't believe that anyone, after only one Canyon experience, can remember much about navigating the dozens of complicated rapids we'll be facing. For our gang, it'll be like total beginners, learning together to raft white water for the first time. It's not a very appealing prospect, especially when you consider the size and violence of a number of the rapids. According to my research, some of them are among the world's biggest and nastiest! On the other hand, John Wesley Powell and his companions made the first run through the Grand Canyon without any reliable information about it, and of course they had to overcome terrible difficulties, but they made it through in wooden boats."

"At least we know it's doable," replies Walt, "and we're not going to be shooting off a high waterfall, or be swallowed up by the river suddenly flowing into an underground cave, like Indians warned would happen to Powell or to anyone else who tried it."

"Well, we've accepted big challenges before, Walt. What say you? Let's do it and hope our luck holds out."

"Let's go!" replies Walt. "And hope our guardian angels will still be with us."

During the final preparations before launching, Georgie

assigns everyone the job of packing all of our supplies into large, black, waterproof bags. When that's finished, she passes out to each of us a smaller duffel bag for our sleeping bags, clothes and personal gear, and then individual life preservers, with a stern, "Never get on your raft without wearing your life vest!"

By early afternoon, all the bags have been evenly distributed in the three rafts and tightly secured with nylon straps. Everyone feels a sense of excitement as the moment arrives for us to throw on our life vests, clamber aboard the rafts, take our assigned places and push off downstream.

I'm positively euphoric at finally getting underway on the adventure that has been such a high priority on my list of goals for so many years. Georgie, facing forward, is on the oars in the lead raft, with Walt, a pleased grin on his face at being able to ride next to Esther, an attractive young single woman, sitting in the stern. I sit in the bow, with a clear view of the river ahead.

Acting as oarsman in the second raft, one hundred feet behind us, is Georgie's husband, Whitey. He is a short, tight-lipped man, whose nickname comes not from his surname but from his white "butch" haircut. With him is a charming married couple, Ed and Audrey Lawrence, and Paul, a stern-faced, thirty-year-old businessman with long black sideburns.

Tom, paddling the third raft, is a forty-five-year-old barefooted vagabond from Northern California with a muscular build and wearing nothing but a red bandana on his head as a sunshade and a pair of lime green swim trunks. Seated behind Tom is a middle-aged couple, Lowell and Lois Adams, with Paul Anderson of Riverside, California, in the front.

We move swiftly on a vigorous current, with only the sound of the dipping paddles breaking the silence. Four miles downstream we float underneath the shiny steel span of Navajo Bridge, 425 feet above us, over which passes Route 89, the "Royal Highway of the West." This is the last crossing over the Grand Canyon and also the last construction we'll see for eighty-seven miles.

Beyond the bridge, the current gathers momentum as the canyon narrows as a result of being bracketed by rugged, two-thousand-foot, sun-reddened cliffs of shale, sandstone and limestone. The strong current makes paddling unnecessary, so we coast along, quietly enjoying the play of sunlight and shadows on the towering cliffs. A hot, sagebrush-scented breeze wafting over us puts me in a dreamy mood. In a reverie, I relive my first encounter with the Colorado.

It happened one summer day when, at the age of fifteen, I hiked eight serpentine miles down the Bright Angel Trail, from the top of the Grand Canyon at the South Rim to the bottom. My intention was to enjoy a close-up visit to the river I planned to explore one day.

As clear in my memory as the moment it happened is the electric thrill I felt at actually standing next to it, hypnotized by my first view of the great Colorado surging before me in all its rich brown glory. It transmitted a siren call to me—a beckoning to leave the world behind and ride with it on and on, all the way to where it enters the ocean. What an adventure that would be! I was impatient to do just that!

The return eight-mile trek back up the Bright Angel seemed endless. It involved ascending to an elevation forty-five hundred feet higher than the canyon floor and took twice as long as the descent. Stifling heat and the countless switchbacks wore me down. Water was the fuel that kept me moving and, fortunately, I carried a large canteen and was able to refill it at springs along the way.

About halfway to the top, a mule train passed me with a tough-looking cowboy type on horseback acting as wrangler, leading a group of park visitors, each one riding a mule. I tried for a little assistance by grabbing the tail of the last animal for a tow, only to have the critter kick back irritably and pull free.

I reached the south rim at dusk, utterly worn out, dehydrated and with sharp stomach cramps. In spite of being slightly decrepit physically, I was on an emotional high from having been able to complete the arduous round trip and more determined than ever to travel through the Grand Canyon on the Colorado River.

The throbbing, freight-train roar of rough water ahead snaps me out of my daydream and back to reality. Georgie calls out, "We're landing at the next beach for a look-see, to get an idea of what we're in for."

We pull in at the next inlet, tie up the rafts and continue on foot over the rocky banks until we arrive at the head of the first rapid of the trip—Badger Creek Rapids. As with the majority of rapids in the Grand Canyon, Badger has been created by the adjacent creek flowing into the river from the right bank. During flooding, Badger Creek sweeps down its narrow canyon, scouring its bed and ramming hundreds of tons of boulders into the river. As it passes over this barrier, the Colorado is whipped into a cauldron of white froth and leaping waves.

With the exception of Georgie and myself, none of our group has ever rafted white water before, and the sight of Badger, a major rapid, with a rating of seven* and a drop of fifteen feet, is frightening to them.

As we huddle together staring at the seething water, Ed Lawrence says, "This stretch of the river just doesn't look possible for us to get through safely."

"I agree," replies Lowell Adams. "I'm thinking this rapid is too rough for our rafts to handle."

Hearing this, Georgie responds with a reassuring, "This really isn't so bad. We'll do okay, so let's just enjoy it."

After planning a course through, Georgie advises, "My raft will go through first, then I'll hike back from below and let Whitey and Tom know how to take it."

Esther, Walt and I jump into our raft with Georgie. She paddles out to midstream and lines up for a straight-on approach, following the usual oil-smooth V that funnels the current into the rough water of the rapid. Although it has been three years since I experienced rapids, as we drift downstream I am aroused by the same nervous reactions I felt in my kayak when approaching each of the thirty-three dangerous rapids of the Nile—the sweaty fear, pounding heart and dread of a capsizing. I calm down by reminding myself that many others have survived the Canyon rapids. Also, unlike the Nile, we won't be

---

*The river scale, set up to rate rapids based on their violence, goes from one to ten. A number one rapid is merely a riffle; four, five and six are moderately violent; and seven, eight and nine are heavily violent; ten is the maximum—explosively violent and a major hazard in any kind of boat.

menaced by aggressive crocodiles or hippo along the way.

The broad sweep of Badger is a veritable garden of stone—boulders of every size are dispersed throughout from bank to bank, with waves swirling over and around each one. Just before reaching the first turbulence, the raft drops abruptly as it bounces over the brink of a submerged reef. Instantly, we tighten our grips on the safety rope encircling the raft—one hand in front, the other clutching the rope behind us, for maximum stability. My pulse quickens when I look downstream and see where our present course is taking us. Rearing up directly ahead is the central feature of the entire rapid, a huge standing wave, ferociously churning with violence from the river smashing into a boulder larger than the size of our boat. Georgie paddles frantically in an attempt to dodge around one side or the other of the menace, but is no match for the strong current. "Oh, for an outboard to give us some control!"

We are being swept faster and faster toward the waves, their booming sound matching their fearsome appearance. We face the real possibility of a head-on collision with the monolith, which would result in a disastrous capsizing and in our being engulfed. I have a fleeting impression that we'd all have a better chance of surviving by jumping overboard, away from the danger, and taking a chance in floating through in just our life preservers. That idea quickly evaporates with one glance ahead at the multitude of rock fangs shredding the current to froth beyond.

I think to myself, *We haven't even run our first rapid, and we're already facing a watery grave.* As a defiant gesture of optimism that we are going to live through this crisis, I grab my movie camera and begin filming the last critical seconds of our run, half expecting a lethal dunking in the unswimmable uproar.

Just as it seems certain that we are going to destruct in an inevitable smashup, a minor miracle occurs when Georgie's muscular thrashings with the left paddle, coupled with a forceful deflection of the current to the right, enable us to swerve away from the heaviest turbulence and careen around the right side of the hazard. During our end-run we are hit only with a barrage of smaller waves, but they cascade down, drenching us with cold water and nearly swamping the raft. With whoops of triumph, we reach calm water at the end of the rapid to a chorus of rebel yells from our companions, who have been pacing us on shore and observing our entire dangerous ride. Following instructions from Georgie to stay as close to the right edge of the main channel as possible, Tom and Whitey and their passengers return to their rafts and have an exciting but undramatically successful navigation through Badger. "Well, that's one down, only 160 more rapids to go!" I say to no one in particular.

Surviving our first test with a major rapid, we camp nearby on a wide beach of sugar-fine sand. After a dinner of chili beans and bread, we fan out, spread our sleeping bags and turn in, the throaty roar of Badger lulling us to sleep. With no city-shine or pollution to obscure it, the night sky is majestic with a vast display of diamond-brilliant stars.

We arise at dawn, stiff from sleeping on the unyielding sand. After a light breakfast, we hike up the nearby canyon and fill our canvas bags with clear water from a brook. This saves us from drinking the river water, which is so heavily saturated with silt that it inspired the old expression, "Too thick to drink, too thin to plough."

During the following three weeks, we travel downstream at a leisurely pace toward Lake Mead. We enjoy an intimate communion with the most sensational natural wonder of the world—the Grand Canyon—riding on one of the world's most dynamic waterways—the Colorado River! We laze along in our muscle-powered rafts, with no intrusive outboard motors to disturb the tranquility or pollute the air. We take turns at the paddles for long stretches, at times too absorbed with the stunning panorama of sights around us to even speak, or intrude on an inspiring Zen moment. We are immersed in a kaleidoscope of vibrant colors, from our jet black rafts and yellow paddles to the broad sweep of the cinnamon brown river, enclosed by gigantic rust-red, tan and dark purple cliffs and bordered by feathery green tamarisk trees. Overhead, an expanse of blue sky is dappled with occasional puffs of white cumulus clouds. We pass an endless procession of cliffs and side canyons that form an architectural fantasy of rock formations that resemble castles, temples, fortresses and skyscraper-tall urns, all of them sculptured by eons of wind, rain and by fluctuations of temperature, ranging from scorching to sub-freezing.

The beauty of the canyon is enlivened by a broad range of wildlife. We observe charming little burros on the right banks and stately bighorn sheep on the left. Magnificent golden eagles soar high above us, while great blue herons fish in the shallows along the shores.

There is a small adventure one afternoon when I lead

Esther and Tom on a long hike up one of the narrow side canyons, following a shallow rivulet of water. We finally arrive at a steep rock wall and bypass it by climbing around to the faint game trail above. I've always had a policy, on every hike, of taking a different route on the return trip for variety and to see more terrain. When it came time to return to camp, we head down the adjacent canyon. I'm just about to hop off a sandstone ledge when we hear the sound of a rapid-fire castanet. I quickly pull back as we spot a coiled rattlesnake in the shade of a bush, just a yard away from where I was about to step down. Both my companions are upset by this encounter, but become more nervous when I walk around the snake and immediately startle two other rattlers, lying in the dry grass next to the bush, into vibrating their warning clatter.

So there we stand with three agitated snakes in front of us, each ready to strike if we get too close to them. My friends have never seen one rattlesnake in the wilds before, let alone three. Therefore, they are understandably fearful. They tell me they have always regarded snakes as ugly and detestable. I reassure Esther and Tom, informing them that snakes generally have poor eyesight and are never aggressive except when threatened or provoked. I explain that the rattlers perceive our appearance as a possible menace to *themselves*, and they are stimulated to rattle as a warning for us to keep away.

Seeing an opportunity to help my skittish friends develop a more realistic attitude toward snakes, I pick up a dead twig, step close to the first rattler and carefully press its head down with the stick. I lean forward with one hand extended and grasp the snake around its neck. I position my thumb on one side of the neck, the middle finger on the other side and my index finger on top, with just enough firmness to control the head, but not so tight as to injure the delicate vertebrae.

"Look out, John! You'll be bitten!" exclaims Esther.

Tom, also alarmed, says, "You're crazy, John. You're just asking for it!"

"Don't worry," I reply. "As long as I hold the rattler like this, I'm in no danger of it biting me."

To Tom and Esther, with their lifelong revulsion of snakes, particularly dangerous ones, it appears that I'm being reckless and flirting with disaster in catching the rattler. But years of experience in handling all kinds of poisonous wildlife enables me to do this safely. My first pet snake, at the age of eight, was a three-foot gopher snake. This was followed by a succession of other non-poisonous reptiles, all released into a suitable habitat after enjoying them for a brief time. At the age of twelve, I caught and released my first rattlesnake, a red diamond-back in the Mojave Desert of California. Throughout my life, I have handled many other venomous creatures without being bitten, from scorpions and black widow spiders to Gila monster lizards, from water moccasin snakes in the Okefenokee Swamp of Georgia and the Everglades of Florida, to puff adders and gaboon vipers in Africa.

I sit down on the ledge with the aroused rattler frantically squirming on my lap. With my free hand, I gently stroke its thick coils for a few minutes, until it gradually relaxes and stops struggling. Seeing that I have secure control of its head, and after much coaxing, Esther and Tom feel confident enough to sit next to me and actually touch the snake too, lightly stroking the rough scales on its back and the cool, smooth underside. This is a major breakthrough for both of them, since neither one has ever touched a snake before.

"I can't believe I'm doing this," says Esther. "I wish Mom could see me now. She'd probably pass out. She believes that women have had a natural fear of snakes since the Garden of Eden!"

Tom adds, "If you hadn't been with us, John, I probably would have clobbered all three rattlers with rocks."

"I understand that, Tom," I say. "A lot of people have that same impulse—to kill a snake whenever they encounter one. Of course, you can't allow venomous snakes around a neighborhood, but they are an important part of nature, and with a little caution we can share the wilderness with them safely. After all, they use their fangs and venom only to get food and defend themselves."

With the rattlesnake now calm and not feeling threatened, I set it down on the ground and step back. While the three of us watch, it slowly creeps off into thick brush and disappears. And we continue back down the canyon to our riverside camp.

LIFE GOAL #202: *Film White-Water Raft Trip Through the Grand Canyon*

White-Water Death Trap

O nly three and one-half miles downstream from Badger Creek, we come to the infamous Soap Creek, considered one of the most rampageous rapids in the Canyon, with a drop of seventeen feet and an intimidating rating of eight. As a test of my ability to film from the river, I make a trial run without my camera in our lead raft with Georgie and Walt.

We get thoroughly tossed around in the choppy waves of the rapid, but emerge unscathed and tie up to a boulder on the left bank below. Confident that I can shoot a great film sequence without getting heaved overboard or getting deluged in a barrage of waves, as usually happens when running an eight-rated cataract, I ask Georgie and

Walt to go with me again through Soap Creek in the second raft. Because my life jacket is so bulky, it makes filming awkward, and since the first ride went so smoothly, I remove it for greater freedom.

We launch into the river, one hundred yards upstream, with Georgie on the paddles, facing forward in the middle of the raft, Walt hanging on to the ropes in the bow, and me, with the camera, in the stern. Tapping Georgie on the shoulder, I request, "Please try to follow the exact course you took on the first run. It was perfect!"

"No sweat," she replies.

There is ample time to line up for the same approach as before. We swoop down the smooth-as-a-waterslide V, near the right bank, but plunge into the ugly suckhole at the bottom and hit the "rooster tail" wave in front of it just slightly off center, and we flip upside down. The upset happens so abruptly that I have no time to draw an extra breath for being underwater. One moment I am looking through the camera viewfinder, concentrating on filming our action-packed ride, the next instant I am swept out of the boat into a black tornado of violence, seized in the clutches of a frenzied monster that seems determined to annihilate me. Underwater, Soap Creek Rapid is even rougher than on the raging surface, with a furious washing machine-like action that drags me down into its chilly depths, then spins me around like a rag doll. Without my life preserver, which I had foolishly removed, I am defenseless. With a great effort I'm able to secure my right arm by shoving it under my belt, but the left arm remains free and uncontrollable, with the camera still attached to my hand. I'm unable to shake it off because I had cinched up the leather holding strap as tight as possible, to enable me to hold the camera steady during filming. As I roll and tumble wildly in the turbulence, a surge of current captures my flailing left arm and flings it upwards, causing the Bell and Howell, a heavy chunk of metal bristling with three lenses, to bash me in the forehead, momentarily stunning me. It feels like I have been walloped with a bowling ball. This is like a *coup de grace,* the final death blow, because I was already reaching the end of my endurance *before* being struck.

Dazed and weaker now, with no reserve of strength left to draw from, I realize that my life is coming to an end, with only a glimmer of consciousness between me and drowning. My mind has become so dulled from the pain of the head injury and exhaustion that I begin to lose the "edge" between fighting to survive and passively submitting to what seems like an inevitable fate—with the all-too-familiar feeling that death is rapidly approaching. How easy it would be to just give up and let it happen! I have an overpowering urge to be free from terror, pain and the superhuman effort of holding my breath any longer. My lungs, ravaged from lack of oxygen, feel on the verge of bursting. My heart is banging away in my chest with such force that it feels like it will break through my rib cage at any moment.

Only seconds from drowning, I'm granted a miraculous second chance when a strong upthrust of water sweeps me to the surface, where I fill my lungs and begin to revive. Below the rapid now, I'm carried along by a calm but swift current, weak as a kitten, and still so weighted down by the camera that I'm barely able to keep from going under again. But as my head clears I hear a voice calling out, "Hey, John! There you are!" and through blurred vision make out the dim figure of Tom, standing alone in the third raft, no more than fifty yards downstream. As he back paddles, I quickly catch up to him and am snatched out of the river by his strong hands. I lie in the bottom of the boat, too worn out to speak, except to mutter a hoarse "Thanks!"

Tom paddles us to a landing, about a mile ahead, where we find the rest of the group gathered together on the shore. As I sit up in the raft, there is a cheer of relief at seeing me still alive.

I'm overjoyed at the sight of Georgie and Walt, weary and soaking wet, but obviously in good condition. They sit together on the rocks, next to the overturned raft floating before them. We share a quick description of what happened at Soap Creek. So as to observe and photograph the two raft runs, the group had stationed themselves along the left bank at the beginning of the white water. They were shocked when the second raft, bearing Georgie, Walt and me, capsized in front of them. They watched as my two companions quickly popped to the surface and grabbed the rope attached to the side of the raft, but were alarmed when I didn't appear with them. When the raft had floated far downstream and I still hadn't surfaced, they feared the worst—that I was either trapped under the raft or I had drowned and had been carried away. Tom then rushed back to the third raft, still beached above the rapid, and made a solo transit through and beyond in hopes of finding me. If my friend had passed by Soap Creek less than a minute earlier, he would have traveled too far downriver to have been able to spot me in the water. Overwhelmed by the force of the current, with no energy left, I would have gone under for the last time. The timing of Tom's appearance and his rescue was, for me, the critical difference between living and dying—a perfect example of both of us being in the right place at just the right time!

LIFE GOAL #460: *Enjoy the Sport of Snowmobiling*

The Human Cannonball

The sport I look forward to most each winter is cross-country snowmobiling. Astride a swift and powerful snowmobile, I love meandering through the vast uninhabited forests and snowfields of northern Utah's Wasatch Mountains. Though I prefer the serenity of cross-country skiing or travel on snowshoes, the snowmobile enables me to cover far greater distances and truly "get away from it all" in a fraction of the time it would otherwise take me. It is the purest kind of escapism for me when I leave the stressful environment of urban living to explore the trackless, snowbound wilderness, stopping frequently to absorb the peaceful solitude. On one sunny but frigid March day, I cruise along for hours through the tall trees and over moguly snowfields without any particular destination. Though the engine has an effective muffler on the exhaust, I travel at half throttle to further minimize the noise. Except for a few raucous crows flying overhead, there has not been a living creature in sight all morning.

When I spot a perfect rest stop atop one of the high ridges of a frosted mountain, I head toward the base. To provide maximum traction, I shift my weight as far back as possible and make a long, running approach at full throttle to build up speed. From the foot of the mountain, I race straight up the steep slope with a stimulating sense of speed and power, and my momentum carries me to the crest of the ridge without faltering or slipping back. Once at the top I switch off the engine and sit for an hour, scarcely moving, savoring the silence and the beauty of the morning. I gaze out over the wintry panorama of endless pine and aspen forests and the glistening mountains cloaked in heavy snow, and I feel a profound spiritual response to the unspoiled world spread out below me. Far from the distractions of civilization I experience a period of calm meditation that fills me with a deep inner peace. I am always spiritually renewed whenever surrounded by pristine wilderness, anywhere in the world.

When I begin shivering from the cold, I start the engine and swoop down the face of the mountain at top speed. A few miles later, I am whisking along at forty miles an hour across the frozen surface of a treeless plain when I notice a long, low rise ahead. It appears that I can skim over the top of the knoll without any difficulty, as there is a smooth expanse of packed snow leading up to it. Even so, I cautiously throttle back to reduce speed. But just as I have almost reached the top, the front of the snowmobile suddenly crunches into a hidden depression under the snow and crashes into a solid rock wall.

The abrupt stop catapults me into the air as if I had been shot out of a cannon. I soar above the ground for several seconds, unintentionally executing a perfect somersault, then crash onto the snow with a bone-jarring thud that knocks the wind out of me and renders me senseless.

I lay there, wracked in pain from head to heels, trying to catch my breath and wondering how many bones have been broken.

I feel over my body but find no evidence of any fractures or serious injuries. When I sit up and remove my heavy helmet there is blood on my face. As I was ejected from the snowmobile my head had struck the top of the windscreen. The plastic visor of my helmet rammed into my face, opening a cut on the bridge of my nose and bruising my forehead. It is a relief to be able to stand and find I can still walk, though severe bruises on my legs and back make me limp from the pain.

I hobble back to my stalled machine, more than twenty-five feet away. The front of the vehicle is nose down, partially buried in a small pit in the snow. As I examine the scene I discover what had caused the accident. As I was speeding along over the snowfield, the snowmobile had crashed through the crusty surface near the top of the rise and had hit the rocky bank of a hidden stream. I couldn't see the creek because it was completely concealed by a heavy accumulation of snow. What had appeared as a gentle slope, similar to others I had traveled over during the day, is actually a natural pitfall that had instantly stopped my three-hundred-pound machine and sent me sailing through the air. The collision with the stream bank had caused the dangerous heart-stopping flight. If, instead of coming down on cushioning snow, I had landed on ice, or a rock surface or had even hit a tree, the results would have been disastrous.

LIFE GOAL #78: *Free Dive to Forty Feet and Hold Breath Underwater for Two and a Half Minutes*

Bottom-Skimming —An Extreme Sport

A s a natural born aquanaut, I always feel a strong affinity for water in all its wondrous forms. Other than when I am with family or friends, I am happiest when traveling over a lake, down a river, or on or under the ocean as a sailor, explorer, surfer or diver. Many of my fondest memories are of diving in oceans around the world and of getting "close and personal" with dolphins, seals, sharks and whales.

One such memory comes from scuba diving in Darwin Bay in the Galapagos Islands, six hundred miles from the coast of Ecuador. While I am cruising along seventy-five feet below the surface, a pod of twenty-eight adult sea lions suddenly appear and begin performing an incredible swirling choreography of graceful climbs, swoops, loops and rolls all around me. It is like a squadron of fighter planes attacking a lone bomber, except in this situation, the "fighters" are completely friendly and nonthreatening. While diving for lobsters and abalone off the California coast, I remember sea lions approaching me underwater out of sheer curiosity. On one occasion a sea lion even joined me while I was surfing and rode the same wave I was on! A human and an animal, both fun-loving, momentarily sharing the same recreation. But I've never had an experience where an entire pod of sea lions put on such a magnificent performance for me. Fortunately, I preserved the entire encounter on film so I can create an encore performance whenever I like!

During diving excursions, I enjoy a specialized sport that I call "bottom-skimming." This is an oceanic version of "hedge-hopping" in an airplane where one flies at a low altitude over uninhabited countryside. Finding a suitable beach with sizable waves and a rising tide, I don my trunks, diving mask and fins, and plunge into the surf, swimming far out beyond the breakers. Turning toward shore, I take a few deep breaths to saturate my lungs and dive down through the clear water some fifteen to twenty feet to the ocean floor.

Assuming a horizontal position with my arms flattened along my sides, I kick steadily ahead with my fins until I become caught up in the powerful undersea flood of the tidal current surging toward shore. I become a sea creature, feeling an overwhelming yet serene sense of kinship with the dolphins and seals that I have come to love. Both excited and at peace, I am at one with nature, immersed in a current created by the primordial pull of the moon!

I race swiftly over the swirling, bright green sea grass and the black rock reefs, traveling at times mere inches above them. The sensation of speed is accentuated by my closeness to the ocean floor. When I come upon an obstacle in my course—a boulder or rocky outcropping—I lift my torso, dash over the obstruction, dip down the other side and continue shoreward. It is a thrilling sensation.

Nearing shore, I catch a breaking wave on the surface and bodysurf right up to the foamy shallows of the shore. Occasionally on my sweeps, I startle a school of fish, a lone stingray or halibut resting on a sandy area. After several such sweeps, I'm tired and cold, ready to warm up and relax with friends on the beach.

My bottom-skimming adventures are not limited to just the sea floor. Wearing fins and mask, I also have had marvelous fun hurtling along underwater in the fast currents of the Yellowstone, Snake and Colorado rivers. There have been a few dangerous situations with this sport, such as being momentarily trapped in strong undercurrents and whirlpools, getting battered and bruised in scraping over boulders in shallow water. One really close call that comes to mind could have easily taken my life.

The bottom-skimming experience I'll never forget takes place on the Colorado River, near Blythe, California. I am scheduled to deliver a seminar on African anthropology for the students and faculty at the local Palo Verde College later that evening. Arriving in Blythe at noon, I naturally must try out swimming and diving in the nearby Colorado.

Though Blythe has triple-digit daytime temperatures during summer, this is May and the air temperature is a pleasant eighty-five degrees. After following a trail through a dense thicket of rabbit brush and mesquite, I jump into the dark, green river, just below the steel bridge connecting California and Arizona. The water is surprisingly cold at the surface and really chilly in its depths. I dive down to check out the rocky riverbed and find it, at twenty-five feet, too dark and deep for skimming in mid-channel. But moving closer to the right bank, I find much better conditions, good visibility and a warmer temperature. I am in prime skimming territory!

The current sweeps me ahead at a brisk pace, somewhere around eight miles an hour. My plan is to ride downstream for two or three miles, then hike back to my car. It's incredibly peaceful to be transported along in the soothing water at such a swift speed. I am lulled by the current, relaxed and enjoying the constantly changing sights of the riverbed beneath me. There is no need to exert myself other than to rise to the surface and breathe fresh air periodically. Then it happens—just a few seconds after one of my surface breaks and getting back on the bottom, I have a scare that sends the adrenaline through me like a bullet. An apparition appears—a mysterious *something* directly ahead of me. In the dim light, it looks like some grotesque monster with long, menacing tentacles that undulate in the flowing current. The tentacles seem to reach out to grab me and before I know it, they have!

Quickly, I realize that I'm caught up in the leafy branches of a submerged cottonwood tree, floating freely and rapidly along the western bank of the river. The waterlogged cottonwood materializes so abruptly that I have no time to veer around it to safety.

In an instant, the current plunges me into the thickest center of the huge tree, my bare arms and legs getting lacerated by rough twigs and limbs. As I desperately try to resist, the powerful current, formerly my source of recreation, has become my nemesis. It jams me deeper and deeper into the dense growth, flowing so forcefully against my body that I am crushed irresistibly against the larger branches. In struggling to extricate myself, my head becomes caught in a viselike clamp between two intersecting limbs, causing my diving mask to half fill with water. My arms and legs are entangled in the midst of a thicket of smaller branches. Even my large swim fins become enmeshed in the greenery.

I am helplessly trapped and nearing exhaustion. Just a few feet underwater, I'm enveloped in a suffocating cocoon of shrubbery, unable to breathe and barely able to move, with an overpowering surge of panic welling up inside. It all seems like a horrible nightmare. I feel completely helpless, like a moth caught in a spider web—seconds from death. In those frightening seconds, I face the stark reality that my life is slowly ebbing away because I have run out of air. I wonder to myself, *Is this the way I'm going to die?* No doubt, some of my Viking ancestors had a send-off to Valhalla in a burning funeral ship, but I'm still alive and not ready to quit life entombed in a tree!

Then, suddenly, a wave of anger overcomes the panic and lends me the strength that I need to survive. I have just enough left in me to free both my hands and place a firm grip on two opposite branches. Then I kick my legs free and pull my knees under me atop the broad tree trunk. Thus stabilized and with a solid fulcrum underneath me, I give a vigorous push backward against the pressing current, then use its forceful momentum to launch myself forward. I try aiming for a cluster of the thinnest branches, and with the last remnants of my energy, I thrash furiously with my swim fins and burst through the confining limbs to escape what was almost my watery tomb.

I immediately pop to the surface and, with an explosive gasp, release my oxygen-less air. Hastily, I rip off my flooded facemask and let it sink, so that I can also breathe through my nose. I am disoriented by a fit of shivering from fear and cold, and I'm so lightheaded that I feel that any more vigorous exertion will cause me to pass out.

Too feeble to do anything more than remain on the surface, I let the powerful Colorado carry me downstream for several more minutes. At a bend in the river, I crawl out through a break in the salt brush covering the bank on the California side. Still on my knees, I begin retching and coughing, then throw up a copious amount of river water, swallowed during my struggle in the tree. I collapse on a shaded patch of dry grass in a willow grove, too worn out to even remove my tight swim fins, but relieved at last, to feel solid ground beneath me.

While I rest on the warm grass, I become aware, for the first time, of stinging pains all over me. Sitting up, I discover scratches and gouges, some still bleeding, all over my body from neck to ankles—the result of being scraped over the abrasive branches of the cottonwood. The discomfort from these minor wounds vividly confirms the fact that I have really survived—that I still exist. A spontaneous emotion sweeps over me—a delayed reaction to my near-death experience. In a virtual state of exaltation, I suddenly feel like shouting to the sky, "I'm alive! I'm still alive!" I am filled with an inexpressibly powerful feeling of thankfulness for having lived through an ordeal that came within seconds of sending me to the Great Hereafter.

LIFE GOALS #384: *Dive on the Ghost Fleet of Truk Lagoon*

The Deepest and Most Dangerous Dive of All

 uring World War II one of Japan's major naval bases in the southwestern Pacific was situated at Truk Lagoon in the Caroline Islands of Micronesia.

The lagoon is forty miles in diameter, the world's largest, and was created in ancient times by an enormous volcano. It is encircled by a protective 125-mile coral barrier. The Imperial Japanese Navy chose Truk as an ideal natural anchorage for its Fourth and Combined fleets and as a vital depot for transporting supplies from Japan to southern Pacific campaigns.

To shut down this base, a U.S. raid with the code name "Operation Hailstone" was organized. Beginning early in the morning on February 17, 1944, an American aerial attack, consisting of 450 carrier-launched fighters and dive bombers, surprised this armada of Japanese warships and military cargo ships anchored at various locations throughout the lagoon.

After two days of intense bombing, aerial torpedoing and strafing, forty ships were sunk and hundreds of sailors killed and more than four hundred Japanese aircraft had been destroyed in one of the most horrendous military disasters of the war. Ten weeks later, another U.S. attack caught the remnants of the fleet off guard and sent another twenty vessels to the bottom.

From the first time I read details about this huge sunken graveyard of sixty ships called the "ghost fleet of World War II," it became my highest-priority diving destination. Shortly after it was designated a historical monument and undersea museum, I flew to Mauro, one of the eleven sizable islands in Truk, accompanied by a friend, Dr. Ed Mills of Pasadena, California.

We arranged to work out a diving schedule with Kimiuo Aisek, a personable Trukese scuba diver who had witnessed the 1944 air attack as a youth of seventeen. He is the ideal guide for our project since he had memorized the location of several of the largest ships as they sank.

For several days Ed, Kimiuo and I have a wonderful time scuba-diving on fifteen different vessels. We also investigate an intact Mitsubishi "Betty" bomber and a Zero fighter.

One afternoon I am diving alone and lazing along over the coral-studded bottom, seventy-five feet down, when I spot two white-tipped reef sharks, both at least nine feet long, in the distance, moving rapidly toward me in what appears to be a direct frontal attack. My pulse speeds up until I feel the throb of every heartbeat. It seems certain I am about to be chewed up by the toothy pair. My first impulse is to head for the surface as fast as possible, but then I remember from past encounters that sharks approached closer as I headed for the surface but retreated when I bluffed them and dove slowly toward them.

Striving always to be optimistic in any tight situation, the idea flashes through my mind, *I'll wait a few more seconds and then turn my back to them so that they'll bite my air tanks and not me.* This little maneuver proves unnecessary, thank heavens, because the sharks break off the attack when only a few feet away, veering around me and disappearing into the blue depths.

The most exciting of all my dives at Truk comes shockingly close to being the last experience of my life. One sultry morning the three of us set out to explore one of the largest of all the sunken armed merchant ships, the 385-foot *San Francisco Maru*. It rests upright and intact on the bottom at a challenging depth of two hundred feet, the absolute maximum depth any of us wants to attempt, even wearing double air tanks.

Kimiuo takes Ed and me out to the dive site in his motorized launch. We quickly don our gear, carefully adjusting our air tanks, weight belts, swim fins, face masks, waterproof watches and dive gauges. Then we place the mouth pieces of the demand regulators in our mouths, turn on the air valves and test the air flow to make certain everything is operating normally. We then sit on the gunwales of the boat and launch backwards into the calm lagoon.

With Kimiuo in the lead, Ed and I follow the husky Trukese straight down as fast as we can swim, hard put to keep up with his powerful strokes. There is no problem in diving down because our bodies adjust quickly to the increasing pressure. But we are extremely concerned about ascending too fast. If you rise faster than your air bubbles, there is a serious risk of developing the bends, or caisson disease, which produces intense pain and even paralysis or death.

As we plunge down through the eighty-five degree water, slightly cloudy from a heavy concentration of plankton, we have no view of anything but Kimiuo below us trailing a stream of bubbles as he exhales. The light steadily dims as we near the bottom, but suddenly, at 140 feet, after two minutes of diving, there pops into our field of vision the great ship, materializing as a ghostly shape in the gloomy depths.

As we draw closer we can see that she is encrusted with various forms of living creatures—an unbelievable variety of corals, sea fans, algae, sponges, sea squirts and sea hares. Gaudy tropical fish swim leisurely in and out of her open hatches, singly and in schools. Before us is an entire ecosystem of interrelated sea life, the ship providing shelter and food for everything from the microscopic plankton to large, bug-eyed groupers and fierce-looking barracuda hovering nearby.

On the starboard side of the bow, looking like giant toys, are two three-men tanks, chained to the deck and coated with masses of flowerlike orange and green soft corals. A community of colorful tropical fish cruise around the hulk: parrotfish, rudderfish, little clownfish, red squirrel fish and a snapper. Their bright colors provide a sharp contrast to the pale green patina of the ship.

We glide smoothly a few yards above the ship, tracing her entire length from prow to stem, then fin down and follow Kimiuo as he enters an open hatch. We are soon enveloped in total darkness and switch on our waterproof torches. We want to explore as much of the ship as possible but are well aware of the time constraints imposed on us by our great depth and limited air supply.

When I shine my light in the crews' quarters, I am poignantly reminded of the heavy loss of human lives in the sinking of the *San Francisco Maru*. There are skulls and a few bones resting on the floor and some personal possessions of the sailors who had died there: sake bottles, gas masks and books.

We move along in single file, careful not to stir up too much of the thick layer of silt coating everything. In the officers' mess there are still fine porcelain dishes and rice bowls perched delicately on the shelves. I notice with surprise that these are eerily free of encrustations and look clean and ready for use. It is the same with the stainless steel instruments and long glass thermometers in the surgery.

We investigate the holds of the ship and find them still crammed with the weapons of war. There are hundreds of anti–landing craft mines in the forward hold, some reputed to be still alive. Other compartments hold depth

charges, several cargo trucks, and rows and rows of sinister looking torpedoes. There are also eighteen-inch shells
with a range of twenty miles, originally intended for the
enormous guns of Japan's largest battleships, the *Yamato*
and the *Musahi.*

After we pass through the engine room, with its massive
diesel engines, I notice with a start that my air is getting
critically low and that it is time to head for the surface. I
signal to Kimiuo, pointing to my wrist gauge and gestur-
ing toward the surface. Fascinated by the attractions that
we have been encountering, I haven't been paying close
enough attention to the condition of my air supply.

We turn around, still in single file, and begin heading
back the way we had come in, entering the narrow passageway we had followed into the ship. Immediately we
become enveloped in a blinding brown fog of fine sedi-
ment churned up by our swim fins during our passage
inside. The bright beam of my torch becomes useless as
the light reflects back from the silty cloud, producing zero
visibility.

I lunge ahead to try and locate Kimiuo and am relieved
to bump into his extended fins. Ed reaches out his hand
and touches me so that we are able to continue close
together, though totally blind, by feeling the surge of
water from our fins.

The muddy water makes our progress out of the ship
dangerously slow. But Kimiuo finally changes direction,
moving into a narrow crawl space where the water begins
to clear up. The steel tunnel is so cramped that I turn off
my metal torch and just use it to pull me along by digging

into the deck with the handle so I am better able to keep up with our guide, who lights the way ahead.

Both Kimiuo and Ed have ample air remaining in their double tanks, so there is no urgency in their returning to the surface. But I have been breathing in a greater amount of air than they have because of scarred tissue on my lungs from a near-fatal siege of pneumonia when I was a child.

I am in an extremely hazardous position—literally a "tight" situation, sandwiched between two steel decks so narrow that my scuba tanks keep clanging noisily against the bulkhead above me. I have had minor twinges of claustrophobia on different occasions of my life, including being hopelessly lost in the midst of a trackless jungle in the heart of Africa and in a submarine at a five-hundred-foot depth in the Pacific, as well as when negotiating narrow shafts in mines and caves. But never before have I experienced claustrophobia like the overwhelming, suffocating wave of it that sweeps over me as I grope along through the dark bowels of the sunken Japanese ship with my life-support system gradually ebbing away. I begin hyperventilating from terror and panic.

It requires all my willpower to stifle the irresistible urge to dump my cumbersome tanks and get out of the imprisoning crawl space as fast as I can swim. But reason takes hold, I calm down, regain control and continue moving slowly forward toward Kimiuo and his dim light.

We reach the end of the corridor and begin swimming down the port hallway. My panic attack subsides as we emerge into the welcome light of the open sea. I feel tremendous relief until I check my air gauge and see, with dismay, that the needle has moved to the edge of the red zone. This means that I won't have nearly enough air for the essential period of decompression before returning to the surface.*

Without pausing we leave the ship and head for the surface, moving upwards no faster than our air bubbles. I feel deep despair as my air supply becomes exhausted, picturing myself drowning or dying in agony from the bends—the major danger in deep diving.

As we near the launch I feel a great sense of deliverance at the sight of a single air tank hanging fifteen feet down from the launch. I did not know until this moment that Kimiuo had thoughtfully set this up as a precaution while we were getting into our gear before the dive. This is my salvation since I have exhausted the last of my scuba air and have been slowly expelling the remaining air in my lungs while ascending.

With trembling hands I quickly turn on the airflow from the reserve tank, adjust the mouthpiece and begin enjoying the pleasure of breathing freely with no worry about rationing the supply. The interminable decompression the three of us endure, forced to remain immobilized

---

*When breathing compressed air during a dive, the bloodstream absorbs a large volume of nitrogen under pressure. When heading for the surface, you move from a heavier pressure to a lighter one. If you rise too rapidly the nitrogen effervesces through the circulatory system in a foaming stream of tiny bubbles. The same effect is created when a bottle of soda pop is shaken and then the cap removed. The bubbles cause intense pain as they put pressure on the nervous system and concentrate in the joints. During a sufficiently long period of decompression, the froth of bubbles disperses and is absorbed harmlessly.

suspended from the launch rope, is the longest twenty-five minutes I have ever known. I don't mind it at all. It is a delicious feeling to have survived the deepest and most frightening dive of my life!

Yet
this
rer

EPILOGUE

Contrasting the gratitude and relief from living through the twenty-four close-to-fatal experiences was my initial strong reluctance to expose myself again to any hazardous undertaking. From childhood I have thrived on accepting risky challenges, with an urge to go "beyond the beyond." Not as a stunt or ego trip and never as an attempt to arouse admiration or to gain attention. For me, adventure is where you find it and you can find it anywhere! It has always been the spice of my life, and to succumb to a risk-free, "play it safe" existence would have been unthinkable. The exciting rush whenever I'm engaged in the midst of a dangerous activity feels like an exuberant *celebration of life* with a "hot damn" enthusiasm that intensifies the joy of being alive.

after several of the traumatic escapes described in book, there has been a deep-seated fear that hained: an inclination to avoid anything that reminded he of the original disaster. An encounter with any of them was enough to arouse an emotional reaction that included a dry mouth, rapid pulse and the urge to make a quick getaway. These accumulated fears read like a catalog of neuroses that were in urgent need of psychotherapy. Here are a few examples: after the terrifying climb down the face of the Catalina cliff, for months I avoided returning to one of my formerly favorite sports—rock climbing. Just the sight of a steep mountainside set off internal alarms. As a result of several near-drownings, I was left with a residual fear of river rapids, heavy ocean surf and of underwater exploring. From the capsize on the Nile with the puff adder and, later, of being bitten by a five-foot diamondback rattlesnake, I felt an atypical anxiety whenever I was around snakes. After the airplane crash, a dread of flying persisted. And from the shockingly narrow escape in Truk Lagoon, I suffered a suffocating claustrophobia whenever entering a cramped space, whether an elevator or even a closet.

I was afflicted with post-traumatic stress disorder, the kind of psychological condition experienced by people exposed to excessive stress from war, major accidents and catastrophes, or, as in my case, from terrifyingly close encounters with death.

Unfortunately, when fear runs your life, you begin to withdraw into yourself. Personal development is inhibited. When fears are not confronted, conquered and cast out of the mind, they can sometimes escalate into an anxiety neurosis, and, ultimately, into a debilitating phobia that can seriously disrupt a balanced lifestyle.

During most of my adventures, the mild symptoms of fear I have felt, the accelerated pulse and respiration and the sense of danger, only served to heighten the excitement and enjoyment, and they quickly passed with no lasting effects. This was because I had freely *chosen* to engage in the sports and professional activities involving hazards.

But when physical circumstances caused me, involuntarily, to lose all control and thrust me to the brink of death, it was always emotionally devastating, and terror became deeply implanted in my psyche. Until each terror was exorcised, I missed out on many enriching experiences.

Clearly, I had to face and liberate myself from each fear. I accomplished this by first of all, acting on the old cowboy advice I learned the hard way as a teenage cowboy working on my uncle's cattle ranch: "If you get throwed, get back on the horse and ride again!" In other words, do again the thing that caused you fear, and thereby render it harmless. Also I followed the maxim I had composed in high school, "To fear is to fail. To dare is to do!" In short, I returned to the pleasures of rock climbing, surfing, white water running, scuba diving and even aerobatic flying. My anxiety when around snakes was dispelled by having a large python as a pet and by once again catching and releasing venomous reptiles in Africa and the United States. But this time, I exercised much more caution and better judgment while engaging in each of these adventures.

Admittedly, there was a feeling of nervousness in the beginning. But by starting out slowly, just easing into each formerly frightening activity, confidence steadily increased, skill was regained and eventually the old feelings of enjoyment were restored. When caught in a tight or perilous situation, fear can be a real asset—a positive force simply by transforming it with minimal mental discipline, into pure excitement. This enables you to concentrate the burst of energy that fear generates into an extra boost of strength, making you better able to cope with any fear-producing challenge, whether having to speak before an audience or overcoming a fear of flying.

Because my close calls have made me value life so deeply, I am emphatically opposed to anyone risking their life or health unnecessarily. Based on years of personal experiences, I offer the following suggestions in hopes they might be helpful to anyone wanting to become active in recreation or sports that involve risks: It is important to become physically fit before taking up any sport; professional instruction is essential before engaging in technically demanding sports; consistent practice will build up skill and improve judgment; never attempt actions beyond your skill or experience; always stay in control; never show off or be an exhibitionist; avoid extreme sports, as too often even the most experienced athletes suffer permanent injuries or are killed performing these; and always wear the proper safety equipment. By observing these basic recommendations, dangers and the threat of painful injuries are greatly reduced.

My dear parents never doubted that the main reason I

had survived so many nearly fatal experiences was simply because I had an unfulfilled destiny yet to follow before my time to die could happen. This unshakable belief, through the years, sustained the faith that their adventurous only child was going to live through every danger until his "mission" in life had been completed. I never tried to dissuade them from this conviction since it was a great comfort to them, but I believe—besides a lot of good old-fashioned luck—it was more realistic to attribute my survivals to these sources:

1. A dominant love of life, coupled with an iron-bound determination to overcome every obstacle in order to continue living.
2. Excellent physical condition from my lifelong practice of eating a varied and moderate diet, a consistent physical exercise program and, importantly, from never having been a drinker, smoker or a user of any kind of drug.
3. An inexhaustible well of spiritual strength to draw from. This was the result of being raised in a Christ-centered home by parents who practiced, on a daily basis, the principles of Christianity, not "church-ianity." Spirituality was continually recharged over my lifetime through a close relationship with wilderness, animals domestic and wild, and by associating with admirable people throughout the world who were nonmaterialistic and spiritually inspiring.
4. The use of visualization. During a physiology course I took as a freshman at the University of Southern

California, our professor told the class something I never forgot: "The most wondrous thing in all creation weighs only 2¼ to 3¼ pounds—the incredible adult human brain." This living computer, superior to any nonliving manmade device, is composed of ten billion interconnected neurons or brain cells, capable of storing trillions of bits of information. It is the center that governs every function of our body. The intellectual agent of the brain, the mind, enables us to think, reason, remember, etc. I had learned from experience how to tap into mind power for healing, reducing stress and creating mental images. I used the technique of visualization only sporadically, finding it helpful in my university studies for memorizing large amounts of material. But later it became an important lifelong habit that has been invaluable to me in every imaginable way.

APPENDIX A

Additional Life Goals Accomplished

Climb:
Mt. Agung (Bali)
Mt. Hood (Oregon)
Devil Mountain
    (Venezuela)
Mt. Olympus (Utah)
Paricutin (Mexico)
Timpanogos (Utah)
Mt. Aso (Japan)

Explore Underwater:
Galapagos Islands
    (Ecuador)

Cozumel (Mexico)
Majuro (Marshall Islands)
Crystal Springs (Florida)
Port Limon (Costa Rica)
Shark's Cove (Hawaii)
Sulu Sea (Philippines)
Truk Lagoon (Micronesia)

Film Wildlife Underwater:
Dolphins, fur seals,
    penguins, sawfish,
    sharks, sea lions, sea
    turtles, stingrays

Visit:

The Blue Mosque
(Istanbul)

Great Buddha of Kamakura
(Japan)

Temple of the Golden
Buddha (Bangkok)

Shwe Dagon Pagoda
(Myanmar)

Houses of Parliament
(London)

Buckingham Palace
(London)

Archaeological
Wonderland of Pagan
(Myanmar)

Island of Mykonos (Greece)

San Carlo Opera House
(Naples)

Doges Palace (Italy)

Golden Temple of Amritsar
(India)

Aborigines of Australia

Ataturk's Mausoleum
(Turkey)

City of Troy (Turkey)

King Tut's Tomb (Egypt)

The Sphinx (Egypt)

Temples of Baalbek
(Lebanon)

Machu Picchu (Peru)

Borobudur (world's largest
Buddhist temple,
Indonesia)

**Visit Cathedrals and
Museums:**

Cologne (Germany)

Notre Dame (France)

St. Patrick's (New York)

Westminster Abbey
(London)

Great Temple of Ramses II
(Egypt)

Rock-cut temples of
Lalibela (Ethiopia)

Lake Tana Monasteries
(Ethiopia)

Axum-City of the Queen of
Sheba

Sacre Coeur Basilica
(France)

The Parthenon (Greece)

Anne Frank's home (The
Netherlands)

Taronga Zoo (Australia)

Hermitage Museum
(Russia)

Basilica of John (Ephesus)

Pompeii and Herculaneum
(Italy)

Colossi of Memnon
(Egypt)
Sydney Harbor Opera
House (Australia)
Catacombs of Rome (Italy)
Medieval city of
Dubrovnik (Croatia)
Kyoto (Japan)
Rotorua Thermal Region
(New Zealand)
Pantheon (Italy)
Arlington Cemetery
(Arlington, VA)

Fly:
Goodyear blimp
F-104 Starfighter
F-15 Eagle
F-16 Fighting Falcon
F-111 Aardvark
B-1B Penetrator

Travel Through:
Corinth Canal (Greece)
Panama Canal (Panama)
Suez Canal (Egypt)
Raft trip through Grand
Canyon (six trips)

**Take My Wife on Cruises
from:**
England to Scandinavia
and Russia
Canada to Alaska
California to Mexico,
Panama Canal and
Eastern Caribbean
Italy to Black Sea
Florida through Western
Caribbean

Excursions on:
Canals of Amsterdam
East African safaris (six)
Cross-country elephant
safari (Thailand)
Trip through Amazon rain-
forest
Grand Canal in a gondola

Miscellaneous Goals:
Experience a nonfatal bull-
fight (Colombia)
Ride an orca whale
Catch a snake
Ride a hydrofoil (Macao)
Parasail
Operate a Jet Ski
Learn to windsurf

Produce a TV documentary
   (twenty-four)
Mush a dog team
Learn to cross-country ski
Present lectures (presented
   numerous to audiences
   at places including
   Stanford University, the
   National Geographic
   Society, *Encyclopedia
   Britannica* headquarters
   and Ohio State
   University)

Swim in:
Crater Lake (Oregon)
Lake Arrowhead
   (California)
Great Salt Lake (Utah)
Lake of the Ozarks
   (Missouri)
Lake Mead (Nevada)
Yellowstone Lake
   (Wyoming)
Roosevelt Lake
   (Minnesota)
Lake Michigan (Illinois)
Lake Geneva (Switzerland)
Lake Kyoga (Uganda)
Lake Albert (Uganda)

Lake Kivu (Congo)
Lake Nasser (Eygpt)
Lake Toba (Sumatra)
Lake Atitlán (Guatemala)

Photograph:
Black panther in Venezuela
Crocodile in East Africa
   and Congo
Giant panda in China
   (Beijing Zoo)
Grizzly bears in Alaska and
   Wyoming
Hippo in east Africa-Sudan
Leopard in Kenya-
   Tanzania
Tiger in Thailand
"Flying foxes" in Sri Lanka
   and Australia (giant bats)

Run River Rapids:
Hozu River in Japan
Klamath River in California
Colorado River Arizona
Salmon River in Idaho

Travel on Rivers:
Sepik (New Guinea)
Xingu (Brazil)
Rhine (Germany)

Rio Napo (Ecuador)
Rio Dulce (Guatemala)
Seine (France)
Nanga and Gat rivers
  (Sarawak)
Acanán (Venezuela)
Rio Coco (Nicaragua)
Rio Negro (Brazil)
Kagera (Burundi)
Main Salmon (Idaho)
Irrawaddy (Myanmar)
Mekong (Vietnam)
Menam (Laos)
Suwannee (Georgia)

Visit U.S. National Parks:
Bryce Canyon (Utah)
Carlsbad Caverns
  (New Mexico)

Channel Islands
  (California)
Crater Lake (Oregon)
Denali (Alaska)
Glacier Bay (Alaska)
Grand Teton (Wyoming)
Great Basin (Nevada)
Mesa Verde (Colorado)
Petrified Forest (Arizona)
Virgin Islands (U.S. Virgin
  Islands)
Yellowstone (Wyoming,
  Montana, Idaho)
Yosemite (California)
Zion (Utah)

APPENDIX B

What Are Your Life Goals?

I hope that some of the adventures have struck a chord with you and enable you to know that you can achieve any goal you set your mind to. The key is to create a clearly defined mental picture of each of the goals you want to achieve, then maintain a strong determination to accomplish each one of them. My fulfilling life began with a simple list. Yours can too!

Personal Goals

_____

_____

_____

_____

_____

Educational Goals

_____

_____

_____

_____

_____

_____

_____

_____

_____

_____

Travel Goals

_____

_____

_____

_____

_____

_____

_____

_____

_____

_____

_____

APPENDIX C

Goal Setting and Achieving

When I was ten years old, during frequent hikes and on camping trips with my parents, the birds, reptiles and animals I encountered made me eager to be able to accurately identify them and learn details about each one. Encouraged by an enlightened fifth-grade teacher, Mrs. Keenan at Wilshire Elementary, I began visiting the school library and eventually, the well-stocked local public library, where I enjoyed reading various illustrated children's books on nature and wildlife. By the seventh grade, I was addicted to the joys of reading, to the point of preferring to miss dinner rather than a good read. I had expanded my interests to reading books and magazines on a broad variety of subjects, including biographies of explorers, world geography and adventure travel. My favorite magazine was *National Geographic*. I would devour each issue from cover to cover, as I still do today.

The most marvelous gift I had ever received came on my fifteenth birthday, when my parents surprised me with a complete set of *Encyclopedia Britannica*. Reading extensively in each of the twenty-four volumes opened up the world for me as never before—an inexhaustible treasure house of fascinating information, covering every conceivable topic, that stimulated my interest in countless other subjects.

From the extensive reading came, primarily, the ideas for the dozens of goals that were included on my teenage Life List that I was committed to achieve: rivers to explore, mountains to climb, exotic places to visit, contributions to make, skills to develop. To date there have been a total of 111 goals fulfilled out of the original 127 on the list, *and* an additional four hundred goals accomplished from other subsequent lists.

Even though set up as goals many years before, I have finally succeeded in recent times in accomplishing more milestones, including: studying and filming Sepik River tribes in Papua New Guinea; cross-country skiing on the Grand Mesa of Colorado; visiting the Hermitage in St. Petersburg in Russia; mushing a dog sled pulled by a team of magnificent Siberian huskies in the winter wonderland of California's Sierra Nevada mountains; transiting the fabulous Panama Canal; swimming with and feeding the amazing stingrays of the Grand Cayman Islands; and flying on simulated combat "dog fight" missions in the Navy's F-14 Tomcat, the Air Force's F-15 Eagle and the F-16 Fighting Falcon.

Working on goals continuously since my teenage years has been immensely rewarding. The numerous goal-setting lists have been a daily blueprint for reaching toward an even more meaningful life and a higher level of happiness, growth and success. Yet few of these ambitions would have been realized without first *writing them down,* then *creating a plan,* carrying out *a period of preparation* and *persisting* in reaching a successful completion of each of the now more than five hundred goals. This whole process was driven by an undiminished passion to succeed. I didn't realize it during the creation of my original list, but I began programming my mind for success by *visualizing myself* actually performing each goal, whether it was traveling down the Nile River, joining the air force, going to sea in the Merchant Marine or visiting the Great Wall of China.

Everyone has dreams of accomplishing unusual things in life, but surveys show that only three to five out of every one hundred individuals, young or old, have any kind of system to reach their goals. Dreams are nothing more than frustrating fantasies until actions are taken to make them come true. This can be best achieved by following a lifetime program of setting, concentrating on and achieving goals. A *wish list* should be turned into a *goal list,* then a *"To Do" list,* and finally, *a list of accomplishments.*

Where there have been no worthwhile goals realized along the way, the future too often ends up with disappointment and a lack of satisfaction. Besides enabling us to fulfill desires and interests, goals are of paramount importance in attaining an ideal balance in our lives, specifically by devising strategies to improve:

Health

Physical: Reaching optimum weight and fitness by a healthy lifestyle; where there is an addiction, breaking free from the tyranny of smoking, drugs and alcohol.

Emotional: Reducing stress, fear and depression; expanding friendships and social activities; indoor and outdoor recreation; volunteering for community projects; not harboring grudges, hatred or envy.

Spiritual: Strengthening spirituality by weekly attendance at church, synagogue or mosque; increasing appreciation for great music, art, poetry and literature; developing a close relationship with the natural world and its creatures.

Interpersonal Relationships

Improve by "mending fences"; resolving conflicts, misunderstandings and animosities; creating more quality time to foster family ties; expressing tolerance and compassion for those different from you; having the courage to sever a relationship with someone who is negative and makes you feel depressed and demeaned when in their presence.

Education

Earn a high school diploma, a college or graduate degree, or graduate from a specialized training school; take night courses at a local community college; attend seminars and lectures to improve professional skills and knowledge.

Cultural Development

Improve by watching less TV and increasing reading of intellectually stimulating, motivating and inspiring books and magazines; periodically attending concerts, operas, ballet performances; visiting museums and art galleries.

Financial Security

Create financial security by refusing to "live on plastic," using self-discipline to reduce or wipe out all sources of debt; postpone immediate gratification to enjoy a more secure future; sound, diversified investing based on intelligent research and investigation and reliable advice from professional sources with a proven track record of success.

In conclusion, the most profitable investment you can ever make is not in stocks, bonds, real estate, precious metals or antiques—the most rewarding investment you can possibly make is *in yourself*. In your health, your relationships, your education, cultural development and in your efforts to reach the highest potentials of your personhood.